A GROUP OF FRENCH CRITICS

A GROUP

OF

FRENCH CRITICS

BY

MARY FISHER

Essay Index Reprint Series

BOOKS FOR LIBRARIES PRESS
FREEPORT, NEW YORK

First Published 1897
Reprinted 1971

Library of Congress Cataloging in Publication Data

Fisher, Mary, 1858-
    A group of French critics.
    (Essay index reprint series)
    "First published 1897."
    1. Criticism--France. I. Title.
PQ67.A2F5 1971   840.9   73-37155
ISBN 0-8369-2496-7

PRINTED IN THE UNITED STATES OF AMERICA
BY
NEW WORLD BOOK MANUFACTURING CO., INC.
HALLANDALE, FLORIDA 33009

PREFACE.

"MANY names, many things," says Villemain, "are destined to be effaced in
the progress of the world, and what is discovered or reinstated through the taste for
historical research must often be lost again
in the continual increase of our intellectual
stores. Let us honor, however, all scrupulous, free research that restores a character
worthy of memory, brings into new light a
truth long misunderstood, or points out to
us, in whatever epoch it may be, the nobleness of works of genius and the unalterable
value of devotion to knowledge."

The wish to introduce to the English reading public a group of French critics who merit
of the world the honor that Villemain ascribes
to scrupulous, free research, has led me to
publish this volume. But I have been impelled to this work by more than a mere
wish. I feel that we owe to those who have

instructed and charmed us and developed
our taste, at least the recognition of gratitude, and that if it be possible to extend
their influence, we owe it to the public to
do so. In a close study of these acute critics, whose broad, impartial criticism is based
on deep, indulgent knowledge of humanity,
I have found a teaching that it seems to me
good for us to listen to, and good not only
for us but good for posterity; a teaching
which I, for one, am thankful to have heard.
Summed up briefly, the teaching of these
critics is, that agitation is neither action nor
force; that the revolutionary spirit is, for
the most part, the spirit of youth and dis-
content, and not necessarily the kindling of
patriotism or of righteous anger at the sight
of injustice; that true literary criticism is
founded on scientific psychology; that the
morbid nature-worship of certain minds is
the result of irritated egotism; that the proper
subjects of art and of science are not necessarily identical; that what is true in the latter
may be neither true, beautiful, nor acceptable
in the former, because true art has to do
with the normal not with the abnormal, with
beauty and health not with deformity and
disease; and, lastly, that we are in sore need

of the substitution of healthy, rational ideas in life and literature for morbid and false ones.

I have had yet another wish in mind in the publication of this work, and that is a desire to do justice to a side of French character and French literature that appears to be unrecognized by the general world outside of France. The French are grown used to having the best in them ignored; they are accustomed to hearing themselves called wholly frivolous and pleasure-loving, and their literature characterized as a literature of the sewers and gutters. In the consciousness that these are not correct statements of the facts, they can quietly ignore them, but we need to know better. In a severe article on Mr. George Saintsbury's "Short History of French Literature," Edmond Scherer says: "Mr. Saintsbury shares a caprice common to many of his fellow-citizens, but which is unpardonable in him. He knows all our blustering writers, — those who acquire notoriety by affectations, by coteries, sometimes by scandal. He is familiar with the opinions of second-rate journals and adopts them with confidence. But, on the contrary, wherever there is any originality, any native manner of writing that is pleasing to cultivated minds, it escapes him. He ignores Maurice de Guérin and the two most valuable acquisitions of modern times to our epistolary literature, Mme. de Rémusat and Doudan. Fromentin, the rarest, take it all in all, of our contemporaneous writers, the most interesting, the most enigmatic, the most personal, — Fromentin is not even mentioned in Mr. Saintsbury's pages."

Like Mr. Saintsbury, most of us know French literature through the blusterers. It is a tardy justice, but it is some justice, to contemporaneous French literature and character to introduce to English readers, in these critics, calm, widely-read, mature, and wise, the representatives of the France that survives her revolutions. I feel, however, that the necessities of my task have not always permitted me to do justice to the critics themselves. In selecting passages for translation, I have had to bear in mind the fact that I am writing for English readers only, and must choose subjects of criticism with which they are familiar. But a critic can never so far divest himself of his nationality that he can do his best work on foreign ground. He is strongest always where he is

at home.   Therefore in order to do as much
justice as possible to the critic and at the same
time to interest the English reader, I have
for the most part selected such criticisms as
bear upon French authors who have an inter-
national reputation, and on such subjects as
are of universal and permanent interest.   M.
Scherer is known to English readers through
Mr. Saintsbury's translation of his criticisms
on English authors ; but in these criticisms
Scherer is by no means at his best, is even
feeble at times.   S. M. Girardin's " Lectures
on Dramatic Literature " have, I think, been
translated.   The remaining critics, Bersot,
Doudan, and Gustave Planche, so far as I
know, have been little more than mere names
to English readers, and I trust that I may
have been fortunate enough to make them
much more than that to future readers.

                                                    M. F.

CONTENTS.

A GROUP

OF

FRENCH CRITICS

---◆---

I.

INTRODUCTION.

THE French mind loves light and warmth.
It is content to look only in daylight
for what it wishes to see, and it troubles itself
little about what the darkness conceals. In
this respect it differs notably from the Teu-
tonic or the Anglo-Saxon mind, that loves to
pierce the shadows of the unknown and people them with the chimeras of the imagination. The Frenchman likes to feel the solid
ground under his feet; the German is reputed
to love the kingdoms of the air; and the
Anglo-Saxon is wholly content neither with
the one nor the other. From these national
characteristics proceed what we call mysticism

in German literature, the idealizing tendency in English literature, and materialism in the literature of France. Thence proceed, too, the natural antipathy between France and Germany and the sympathy of the English mind with German rather than with French literature.

But the quiet and steady progress of science, the slow assimilation of its facts, its spirit, so wholly opposed to that of pure speculation, are gradually bringing about a better understanding of the attitude of the French mind and a larger sympathy with its positivism. But in all revolutions, there is an embarrassing transition stage, in which, in our efforts to adapt ourselves to new conditions, we are the victims of many fruitless and unhappy experiments. We do not learn at once that that which appeals to our senses and inclinations in the strongest manner is not always that which appeals to what is highest in us. Like children who snatch at gaudy, rattling toys, we lay hold of the startling and ear-splitting, only to grow tired of glare and noise and disgusted with emptiness and insufficiency. We ought never to forget that it is not the thoughtful, the solid writers of a nation, that first find a hearing and favor in foreign countries. The

shriek is carried quicker and farther than
the simple, low voice whose message must
pass from mouth to mouth in order to be
heard. And so it happens that in our efforts
to transmit something of the French spirit,
we have caught, first, at what Scherer calls
the "blusterers," and ignored the strength of
the nation's literature. It is time that we
were learning where that strength lies in contemporaneous literature. It lies not in the
ephemeral productions of the modern Parisian
school of fiction and poetry, but in the writings of a body of critics, the coolest, wisest,
and most discriminating that have appeared
in any literature. This critical roll is a long
one, and among other names includes such
as Sainte-Beuve, Villemain, Alexander Vinet,
Eugène Geruzez, Ferdinand Brunetière, Émile
Montégut, Gustave Planche, Silvestre de Sacy,
Saint-Marc Girardin, Ernest Bersot, and Edmond Scherer.

With the exception of Sainte-Beuve, Saint-
Marc Girardin, and Edmond Scherer, who
have been partially translated into English,
these critics for the most part are either
mere names or are wholly unknown to the
great majority of English readers. Selecting
from among them, Scherer, Bersot, Girardin,

Planche, and adding Doudan, whose critical work was chiefly conversational and epistolary, I have tried by careful study of these critics, to produce a volume for those who regard literature as something more than recreation; who believe that it has its standards, its recognizable principles of good and evil, as well as anything else that concerns humanity, and who wish to know them in so far as they can be known by familiarity with the opinions of acute and large-minded critics who have made it their life-work to see clearly into men and things.

The great task of modern literature is to preserve the ideals of civilization and at the same time to keep them in harmony with the revelations of science. Rationalism has invaded literature as well as theology. We are no longer satisfied with a divorce of heart and head. We wish to think and believe as well as to feel. The poetry that satisfies a scientific age must know how to invest a fact with a charm; the fiction that satisfies it must be founded on a knowledge of life and humanity as real and as exact as the engineer's knowledge of the principles he puts into play in his management of the locomotive he guides. But this knowledge requires long and searching study and wide and varied experiences. It does not come by inspiration alone. Without the severe and exact training that belongs to scientific knowledge, we shall have pseudo-scientific superstitions and pseudo-scientific chimeras substituted for the old-fashioned superstitions and chimeras of fairyland and mythology. This is what has really happened in fiction. The great popularity of the so-called realistic school is partly to be accounted for by the fact of its apparent revelations of scientific laws with regard to human nature. "Virtue," says Zola, "is a product like vitriol and sugar;" or "Inheritance has its laws like gravity." That may be true : but as Georg Brandes remarks: "We know the laws of gravity, but as good as nothing of the laws of inheritance." So, too, we may know the conditions necessary to the production of vitriol and sugar, but there is no science of human chemistry to give us the molecular changes necessary to the production of virtue and vice. But the realistic school pretends to know the principles of such a chemistry. It has its system. It has badly digested Darwinism and the theories of the new school of criminal anthropology as set forth by Lombroso, and it uses a scientific jargon that appeals to the modern demand for explanation. The great public, like children who are satisfied with *any* answer to their questions, so long as it pretends to be an answer at all, greedily swallows the presumptions of the realistic school in order to satisfy its curiosity, and adopts the mistakes of its charlatan guides in supposing that because science reveals the social origin and evolution of some of our noblest sentiments, therefore these sentiments being purely artificial in their character deserve neither recognition nor respect, and the baser natural inclinations are to be preferred and followed instead. In no direction has this error made greater headway than in the recent frequent attacks upon the institution of marriage, and the degradation of the ideal of love into a purely physical attraction. Granting that love taken in the ideal acceptation of the term is the product of a higher civilization and was unknown among the ancients, it is none the less a reality because all are not capable of it, and none the less of a noble and lofty character. Evolution of sentiment is certainly as noble and real a thing as evolution of matter. Civilization has worked out monogamy as her highest ideal and a departure from it would be a step backward into barbarism. It is impossible that in so close a union as that of marriage, there should not arise at some time that mutual irritation which comes from imperfect sympathies and a clash of interests and wills. It is impossible, too, that a union often contracted in a moment of youthful folly and illusion should not sometimes bind together those who should never have met, and for whom a divorce is the only legitimate reparation of a terrible mistake. But it is nevertheless true that a very great deal of the irritation and restiveness felt under the marriage yoke, by women in particular, is caused by that morbidly sensitive nervousness and hysterical egotism that are induced by unwise education and an idle, luxurious life. Our less refined ancestors were like children in their domestic relations; they quarrelled and kissed, forgave and forgot, and hand in hand went " down the hill thegither." Our modern married people nurse their wrath to keep it warm; they ruminate over their disagreements, exaggerate their importance, read exciting literature spiced with similar experiences, imagine themselves doomed to life-long wretchedness, and immediately begin to realize their anticipations. By far the greater part of the tragic-marriage fiction that has been flooding Europe during the past decade has come from the pens of women. It is the shriek of a petulant child, spoiled by over-indulgence and wholly engrossed in its own wilful desires; it is not literature.

Modern fiction, in attempting to be scientific, errs in another direction : it confounds psychology with pathology, which are two very different things; it gives us details that belong to medicine and the sick room, and not to literature and art. It uses its powers as would the botanist who should neglect the flowers and trees around him and devote all his study to nut-galls and hideous excrescences on bark and leaves. The description may be faithful, the language captivating, the interest well sustained, but after all, we have only got a nut-gall when we might have had an oak. " All that is true in psychiatry," says Lombroso, " is not acceptable in art. There is no doubt that exaggeration of truths is harmful to literature. The true is not always the beautiful, and there are moral abysses which literature in the name of art has no right to explore."

But it is these moral abysses which much

of modern fiction seems bent on exploring. It seeks its heroes among criminals and its heroism in vice. It pretends to follow scientific teaching, and it leaves out what does not suit its purpose and retains what it likes. In order to understand just what the new school of criminal anthropology teaches and in what essential features the realistic school of fiction departs from its teachings, let us briefly examine the conclusions arrived at by Lombroso. However disagreeable the reading may be, it is necessary to know all that this new school teaches in order to judge rightly, and in order to perceive the full force of the criticism directed against ultra-realism by the critics we have chosen for study. We may believe Lombroso's conclusions or not as we choose, but in view of the fact that he is at the head of the department of medical jurisprudence in the University of Turin and physician to the insane and to criminals in the asylums and prisons of that city, and has examined thousands and thousands of criminals, his opinion is at least worth the attention of those who know the criminal only through newspaper reports of his crime.

In " L' Uomo delinquente," Lombroso, in virtue of the frequent relapses and well-known incorrigibility of criminals, proposes to study the criminal in order to ascertain whether there is anything abnormal in his organic constitution and whether there is a true, natural necessity in crime. He finds that all criminals are not born criminals, but he also finds that there does exist a class of perverted men who are vicious in obedience to their nature; who commit crime for the sake of crime. These men are morally insane, wholly incapable of assimilating the fruits of moral culture, and in the unbridled fierceness of their passions, in the absence of moral feelings and judgments, stand on the same plane that savages do.

Pursuing the methods of physiological psychology, Lombroso begins his investigations by a study of abnormal conditions in plants and animals. The old jurists, he says, spoke of a divine, eternal justice almost inherent in nature. On the contrary, if we glance at natural phenomena, we see acts regarded by us in the highest degree criminal, most widely spread and frequent among the lower animals, offering us, as Renan says, "an example of the most implacable insensibility and the greatest immorality." The fly-catching sun-dews and the Venus' fly-trap offer examples of the first dawn of criminality. These examples become clearer when we pass to the animal kingdom. Jealousy, hatred, strife, and murder follow in the train of natural selection among animals. Ants and termites make a veritable war upon one another. A community of bees will suffer but one queen, and if several appear among them, all but one are killed. Cannibalism, infanticide, parricide, and other revolting crimes find their counterpart among the lower animals. The female crocodile often eats her little ones; cats, rats, and other animals are known to do the same thing, but never in obedience to normal instincts. Veterinary surgeons and persons who have much to do with horses, notice that depraved instincts and vicious habits are associated with cerebral mal-organization. Veterinary surgeons among the French soldiers have given the name of *chevaux à nez busqué* to those horses with a curvature in the forehead near the nose, and these depraved instincts are so far believed hereditary that the Arab takes note of them and will not allow such horses among his selections for breeding. Certain elephants separate from the herd and are morose, solitary, vicious, and dangerous.

They are known as "rogues" among the native Indians, and special hunts are organized for their extermination. After numerous illustrations of further abnormal peculiarities among animals, Lombroso proceeds with a consideration of the crimes and brutalities of savages and then passes on to a discussion of the absence of moral sense in children even of the highest civilization.

It is a fact, he declares, that the germs of moral idiocy and of crime are to be found not by exception but normally in the early age of man's life, just as in the fœtus are constantly appearing certain forms that are monstrosities in the adult. The young child, like the savage, is given to fits of irrational anger, to lying, cruelty, idleness, vanity, jealousy, excessive imitation. In common with savages and criminals, the child is absolutely without foresight. To-morrow does not exist for him. He lives in the present hour, and no event that is not immediate or does not appear so, has the slightest influence over his imagination. To be promised a certain pleasure at the expiration of eight days or at the end of a year is all one to him. The moral sense, however, is one of the faculties most susceptible of being modified by moral surroundings. The child's sense of justice and property and of the rights of others is gradually developed by experience, admonition, and example, and his growing intelligence gives precision to the distinction between good and evil.

The born criminal, on the contrary, never arrives at this distinction. For him, there is no good outside of the satisfaction of his depraved instincts. His very appearance betrays his depravity. The general characteristics of the born criminal are : unusually prominent ears; abundant hair and scarcity of beard ; enormous upper jaw; facial asymmetry; square chin, and broad projecting cheek-bones ; — type, in short, approaching the Mongolian or Negroid. Criminals are also characterized by a marked insensibility to pain. They love to tattoo themselves, and submit to the most painful surgical operations without a groan. This insensibility to pain explains their utter want of sympathy with the suffering of others, for sympathy exists in proportion to physical sensibility. Their sense of taste is dull. They are frequently color-blind. They rarely blush. They are not, however, without affection, but their affections, morbid in character, are in-

termittent and unstable. In place of family
and social affections, dominate with a constant tenacity a few other passions, such as
pride and vanity. They are proud of their
strength and skill, audacity and cunning.
They have an insane desire to be talked
about, which explains the fact that they often
convict themselves in pride of their crimes,
instead of concealing them. To satisfy vanity, to shine, to make a figure in the world,
and to be talked of, are the commonest
causes of crime. A natural consequence of
such restless, unlimited vanity is their inclination to revenge themselves for the slightest
affront. They are lovers of play and drink,
and practise the most revolting forms of
bestial sensuality.

It is a common opinion that criminals are
without religion, but the truth is, that by far
the greater number of them have a sensual
and accommodating religion which makes of
the God of truth and justice a benevolent
tutor of criminals. They rarely believe themselves lost, and die on the scaffold in the firm
conviction that they will open their eyes in
heaven.

Intellectually, criminals are characterized
by their incapacity for continued, assiduous

mental labor; by their singular lightness and
mobility of mind. It is impossible to fix their
attention for any length of time. They are
generally of a cynical, joking humor, laugh
easily and loud, love to rival one another in
slang and in punning, debasing the dearest
and most sacred things by burlesque and
obscenity. They are great liars, and even
when it is their interest to speak the truth,
they are inexact in statement because of
defective precision in perception and memory. Many of them are unable to count to a
thousand. They are great visionaries, are
always going to do the impossible, are
thoughtless, credulous, believers in dreams,
presages, and fatal days. Their ideal is a life
without labor and the unrestrained opportunity to indulge their vicious instincts.

In admitting that there is a class of born
criminals, Lombroso acknowledges the necessity of admitting their irresponsibility. But
in admitting their irresponsibility, he strenu-
ously opposes the weak sentimentality that
excuses them and allows them the liberty of
doing as they please. We do not deny irresponsibility to the mad dog or the venomous
serpent, but we do not the less exterminate
them. The safety of society demands the

incarceration for life, or the death, in certain cases, of the criminally insane.

In his latest contributions to criminal anthropology, Lombroso strengthens his position by taking note of the manner in which the genius of artists has divined and made use of a criminal type before criminal anthropology had studied it scientifically. Michael Angelo gave to his demons animal forms with human faces, characterized by retreating foreheads, prominent ears, and a brutal look of stupidity or idiocy. Raphael Sanzio in his "Last Supper" gave Judas a broad head, contracted eyebrows, and a short, thick upper lip. Delacroix in a series of drawings has treated the different scenes from Goethe's "Faust" and Shakespeare's "Hamlet" and has given to his Mephistopheles the malignancy of feature that belongs to a well-known class of criminals. In short, there was never a great artist that did not adopt for criminals the characteristics that the new school has permanently fixed.

Lombroso then passes on to a consideration of the criminal as depicted in literature. He says that Dostojewski's descriptions in "Casa dei Morti" are so exact that they are really valuable as confirmations of the discoveries in criminal anthropology. He has described in a family of criminals the cold-blooded apathy, insensibility to pain, impossibility of feeling remorse, the exaggerated vanity, idleness, susceptibility to meteoric influences, the childish love of dress and ornament, the impossibility of repressing a desire; — all well noted characteristics of criminals. In one case, he even ventures to say that underlying this criminality there "might be some organic defect, a physical and moral monstrosity unknown to science."

In the above summary, we have the plain, unvarnished truth, the revolting and depressing facts of scientific observation. What place have these facts in art? Do they belong to art at all? Zola and his followers think they do, and that they have a leading place in art. But does he give us the facts as they are? Does he carry out his theory of realism? Let us listen to Lombroso again. Lombroso says that the leading idea of the "Bête humaine" is the born criminal. "But," he adds, "Zola has fallen into singular errors and violates the laws of truth and probability by an atavistic return to the old trick of romancers, who always conceive of fated events as committed in fated places by pre-

destined men and predestined weapons. For
example, in the 'Fortune des Rougons,'
there is mention of a gun with which a
contraband kills a gendarme and which is
used by a rebel nephew against another gendarme and later, in its turn, it kills the assas-
sin, as if destiny were not in the hereditary
instinct, but had been bequeathed to that
unconscious instrument. But Zola's greatest error is not here: it lies in the portrayal
of character. He has depicted drunkards
wonderfully, and even well enough the low
bourgeois of villages and cities, but has not
in my opinion studied the criminal from life.
His portrayals produce on me the effect of
those pale, blurred, photographic reproduc-
tions from oil paintings, instead of from the
living subject. Therefore, I, who have studied thousands and thousands of criminals, am
unable to classify Roubeaud; and a degenerate epileptic like Jacques ought to have
many other defects: a singular violence of
character and unreasonable irascibility, a profound immorality, while, on the contrary, he
appears to be a good man, except in the
ferocious moments that assail him."

There lies the vicious character and the
consequent immorality of Zolaism. It pre-

tends to give the truth, and it suppresses the greater part of it, and in that suppression falsifies what it borrows of reality. It calls itself scientific, and it knows nothing whatever of the broad, calm, impartial spirit of science that tells the whole truth and ignores nothing. It enlists our sympathies for what ought to excite our disgust. It subverts the principles of art by substituting the abnormal for what is normal, and in doing so corrupts the taste and the morals of its readers.

Another favorite subject for pseudo-scientific treatment in fiction, is hypnotism. The vast majority of readers who get their science from novels are under the impression that there exists in certain favored individuals a mysterious power by which they can influence others to do as it pleases them. In an age in which a novel whose plot is based on such a belief can attain unexampled popularity and become for a time the chief theme of pulpits and lecture-rooms, it is not out of place to attempt an explanation of this phase of hypnotism, in a work that wishes to familiarize the public with the principles of true criticism.

We sought in Lombroso, a student of criminals, for what he knew of them, and now we shall seek in Wilhelm Wundt, of the University of Leipsic, an authority in the domain of scientific psychology, for what he can teach us about hypnotism. " At present," he writes, " there exist two forms of scientific superstition: *animal magnetism* and *spiritualism*. The first is over a hundred years old, and dates back to Mesmer, who began his career by publishing a belief in the influence of planets on the human body. Then he taught that a magnet had power over diseases ; that patients could detect its presence in a room, and that they could be healed by the strokes of a magnet. Later he pretended to discover that this magnetic force existed in certain human bodies, that he himself was endowed with the power in an extraordinary degree, and that by rubbing others, he could impart a healing influence. His theory passed to the stage of magic; he declared that he could not only influence persons but that he could magnetize objects, such as iron bars, water in flasks, etc. . . .

" If any one should broach the question how a mythology could be accepted that did not originate in a gray, prehistoric past and in the childhood of national development, but in the light of history under modern conditions of culture and uninfluenced by historic tradition, everybody would shake his head at such a question. Well, the American nation has solved the problem, and its solution is spiritualism. Its development is within the remembrance of every one. About thirty years ago, the first excitement of spiritualism spread like an epidemic over all Europe. The phenomenon of table-turning first appeared; then, spirit-rapping. Then originated the idea that certain persons called 'mediums' could enter into intimate relations with spirits and could communicate to others the thoughts of dead men. Finally it was asserted that the dead could appear visibly in their former bodies. A literature sprang up that claimed to be scientific. Clairvoyants, magnetic healers, sprang up and reaped a harvest from the deluded public. The characteristic form of the superstitions of the present, is that they are spread among the so-called educated classes, while formerly superstitions belonged to the lower class. The peasant is conservative in his superstitions, but on the contrary the 'educated' laugh at the old fashions and riot in the new fantasies just as soon as they believe them to be clothed in scientific garments.

" Investigations have proved that excitable persons, who are usually chosen for magnetic experiments, show all the so-called influences of magnetism *if only they believe that they are magnetized*, and remain completely uninfluenced when subjected to real magnetic treatment if *they do not know that they are so subjected*. The investigation proving this was conducted by a committee of the French Academy to which Benjamin Franklin and Lavoisier belonged. These investigations prove to us that the old magnetic cures were allied to modern hypnotism; that is, they depended on the suggestibility of the subject."

"A noble world governed by grand, unalterable laws, or a little unreasonable world of hysterical mediums, — which?" — this is the alternative which Wundt poses for our belief, and no thoughtful mind asks for a moment in which to deliberate over its choice. It is a noble world, and its laws are grand and unalterable. According to Wundt, hypnotism has no more right to claim to be the true key to psychological laws than dreams, manias, or idiocy. It is an abnormal state into which persons of feeble will-power and morbid, nervous excitability throw themselves under the impression that they are being subjected to the mysterious and unavoidable power of another. " I consider it established," says Wundt, "that the so-called suggestion — that practised by words or by acts to suggest representations — is the principal if not the only cause of hypnotism. The action of other influences, such as fixing the attention upon a determined object, appears to be reduced to this fact, that they facilitate suggestion in provoking a state of consciousness fitted to receive it, or that they themselves constitute a suggestive practice in the sense that they engender the idea of an hypnotic sleep. . . .

" Undoubtedly hypnotism has its value in medicine by aiding physicians to act upon the nutritive functions by suggestion when the malady is a purely nervous one; but hypnotic enthusiasts believe they have found in suggestion a remedy for all the moral maladies from which we suffer. In the future, pedagogues will suggest to a child to be good and obedient until the desired qualities are fixed in the character. Under suggestion, it is said, all artistic works will be produced, from the feats of the acrobat to the less material productions of art. Legends and tales that rational criticism had expelled from history are restored to the dignity of facts worthy of belief. Sleeping Beauty is a cataleptic. Religions are based on hypnotism; their revelations are due to hypnotic suggestion; the tongues of the Apostles are explained in this way. Such are the phantoms of a science gone mad. Of all the relations of man to man that is the most immoral that makes of one the machine of the other. It is the most intolerable of slaveries. . . . Besides, it is a dangerous practice for the health. A constant diminution of the force of resistance of the nervous system ensues, and the subject becomes a victim to hallucinations through his extreme susceptibility to suggestion."

Here again we have the plain, scientific fact. There is no mysterious all-powerful influence emanating from some favored individual, no inevitable submission on the part of another accompanied by inevitable loss of individuality. There is simply a suspension of will-power on the part of a credulous person with an excitable and degenerate nervous system. The influence is not external but internal. The subject is simply the victim of self-delusion.

There are many other scientific truths of a revolting character of which it ought to be noted that the sexless spirit in which they are written and read by scientists is very different from the morbid spirit which in the name of art throws a brilliantly colored, finely-woven mantle of rhetoric over moral ulcers and moral weakness, and persuades unthinking readers that it conceals beauty and health.

The great giants in literature have always recognized this fact. They have chosen the strong, the beautiful, the graceful, and the enduring elements of human character as their chief themes. They have treated with a fine irony or an indulgently contemptuous humor the frailties, the eccentricities, and weaknesses of human nature. Shakespeare does not make the animalism that draws Touchstone to Audrey the theme of his brilliant comedy, but a modern novelist would have suppressed or subordinated Rosalind and Orlando, and in the name of realism and art for art's sake would have made the clown and his doxy the chief subject of treatment.

Everywhere and at all times it is the work of true criticism to expose the rhetorical debasement of the ideal, and this apotheosis of disorder and corruption. True criticism is not the mere expression of an opinion. It

is the search for the faithful reflection of true
life in literature.   It is the careful discrimina-
tion between the false and the true.   It is the
insistence upon law and order in opposition
to anarchy and disorder.

"There are serious problems in human
life," says that acute German critic, Julian
Schmidt, "that no writer can justly avoid.
Has art anything to do with morality?   Whoever judged a landscape by a moral standard
would make himself ridiculous; but where
human actions, principles, and feelings are
concerned, it is natural to judge them by the
standards of morality that belong to men.
The overthrow of an ideal is more dangerous than uncertainty in maxims."   But by
morality, Julian Schmidt does not mean the
"narrow-minded, pietistic, resigned morality," the outgrowth of limitation and fear, but
that morality which makes life richer and
fuller, which is the outcome of the widest,
most fearless culture, and which recognizes
that obedience to law or morality is nature's
fundamental principle of self-preservation.

The criticism of the men whom we are
about to study is of this true kind.   It is
fearless, uncompromising, unrelenting on the
side of morality, yet with no taint of cant or

narrowness. It is touched with the truly
scientific spirit of the age; that is, it is
founded on a profound and intimate knowledge of the human heart, on wide experience,
and a comparative study of national literatures.

It is touched, too, with that indescribable
tang or personal flavor which genius alone
can impart. We feel that there is a man
behind each of these telling, limpid sentences. These clear, solid thoughts are not
mere mouthings; they are growths rooted
and nourished in the inner life of manly
struggle in the darkness towards the light.
I know nothing more helpful than an acquaintance with such men; and in each case,
I have tried to sketch, in rapid yet firm outlines, the personality of the critic, trusting
to the translated extracts from his works to
complete the outlined sketch and give a clear
idea of the quality of his contributions to
literary criticism.

II.

EDMOND SCHERER.

EDMOND SCHERER was born at Paris,
April 8th, 1815, and died in 1889. In
1890, a life of Scherer was published by
Octave Gréard, to whom we are indebted for
the main facts of his biography.

On the side of his father, a Parisian banker,
Scherer belonged to a Swiss family; on his
mother's side, he had English and Dutch
blood in his veins. His father put him into
the Bourbon College, and later, in 1831, sent
him for two years to England to study the
language and literature of that country.

Before going to England, young Scherer
had not been regarded a particularly promising student; but if he were apathetic with
respect to his school-books, he was already
a hungry and omnivorous reader, conducting
his education in his own fashion by consulting the taste and inspiration of the moment,
which is perhaps the best fashion of all

for those who have a native bent towards literature.

In the list of books he was reading at fifteen, are to be found "Manon Lescaut," "Rob Roy," "Cinq Mars," Silvio Pellico's "My Prisons," Courier's "Correspondence," Mme. de Staël's "Considérations sur la Révolution," "Notre Dame de Paris," Sainte-Beuve's "Consolations," "Childe Harold," and Lord Byron's "Memoirs." Even at this early period that which was in later years a marked feature of his criticism, his interest in personality and his appreciation of the refinements of expression, was decidedly strong in him. "The description of manners," says his biographer, "charmed him; poetry intoxicated him, and he tried himself to write verses." The attitude of his mind at this time was sceptical and irreligious. There was nothing in the atmosphere of his daily life nor in the general character of the books he was reading to develop a religious sentiment in him; but his mind was at the same time an impressionable, idealizing mind especially open to all healthful influences, or such as appealed to its love of beauty and order. A daring mind, too, capable of following truth, or what seemed to it truth, through the gloomiest abysses and over the ruggedest pathways in order to reach the serene and sun-bathed heights of intellectual freedom.

The story of the development of such a mind is not an ordinary one; it will be the story of those fierce, silent conflicts of which a rumor only now and then reaches us from some John Bunyan or Thomas Carlyle; a conflict in which few minds are strong enough to engage, and out of which no man comes just what he was when he entered it. He will be either wounded irrecoverably, or he will bear about with him the conscious strength of the victor who knows that henceforth life can offer him no trial that he will be unable to meet. "Edmond Scherer's intellectual evolution," says Édouard Rod, "is one of the richest and most instructive of this century." The whole story of Scherer's life is a story of that evolution, and it properly begins when, as a lad of sixteen, he was sent to England to be placed under the tutorship of the Rev. Thomas Loader of Monmouth.

Monmouth is a beautiful old town in a southwestern county of England bordering on Wales. It lies in a hill-encircled valley just at the point where the rivers Wye and

Monnow unite to flow into the Severn.
Monmouthshire is famous not only for its
picturesque beauty, but for its interesting
ruins, among which Chepstow, Raglan Castle,
and Tintern Abbey on the Wye are the most
celebrated. The name of Tintern Abbey will
recall to every English reader those immortal lines in which Wordsworth has given to
us his joys in Wye's "steep woods and lofty
cliffs," its "waters rolling from their moun-
tain-springs."

Fancy the sensations of an eager-minded
boy, a lover of poetry, with the poet's eye
for beauty in his head, who is suddenly transported from a great city like Paris to a
charming old town like Monmouth, where
in a few minutes he can have fresh, springing
turf under his feet and the murmur of waters
and winds in his ears. The boy has ex-
changed, too, the careless freedom and countless distractions of Parisian life for the placid,
uniform, and methodical home-life of an English parsonage. "The Rev. Loader," says M.
Gréard, "was a rigorist. The first Sunday
that Scherer passed in Monmouth, he had
taken a book, as was his custom, and had gone
for a ramble in the country. On his return,
Mrs. Loader asked him, with tears in her eyes,

never again to distress her husband by such a profanation of the holy Sabbath, and Scherer strictly conformed to that prayer." In winter, he rose between seven and eight, breakfasted at half-past eight, and began his English reading with Mr. Loader at nine. He dined at two, renewed his lessons, which were interrupted by tea at six, after which he continued his reading and extracts until supper at nine, and went to bed between eleven and twelve. In summer, he often rose at four to meet the new tasks he had imposed upon himself. He took up Greek again, and read Blackstone and Burke. With these studies were mingled frequent theological discussions with the Rev. Loader, who often allowed his pupil to accompany him in his pastoral visits to the sick.

This life, so simple and studious, the ever present consciousness of its seriousness, the sad reminder of its brevity by the bedside of the dying, the poetic beauty of his surroundings, the sweetness and charm of the seclusion and intimacy of English home-life, — all these new influences quickly wrought a profound change in this impressionable young mind, and in his diary of that year, 1832, appears this significant record: "25

Décembre, Noël, conversion." He had
sloughed off the sceptical, indifferent, boy-
ish Scherer; he had taken a great stride
forward; he had become a man in the consciousness of a responsibility upon him, and
in the ardent wish to fit himself to discharge
it well. Up to this time, his educational
training had been designed to prepare him
for the law, and on his return to Paris, after
a two years' stay in England, he continued
his legal studies at the University. But
these studies no longer satisfied either his
head or his heart. There was a message
within him shaping itself for delivery, and
he eagerly sought whatever could nourish it.
He found time to attend the lectures in the
literary course. He listened to Saint-Marc
Girardin, Jouffroy, and Victor Cousin. He
read unweariedly. At last, he broached the
subject of his dissatisfaction with the law,
and in '36, he was allowed to go to Strasburg to take a theological course.

Three years in Strasburg gave him a mastery of German. He deepened, too, his
knowledge in Latin, persevering in it until
he could write in it, and then to keep up
his hand, he wrote letters in Latin to his
brother, his professor, and his friends.

Slowly, perhaps unconsciously to himself, the old religious ardor was giving place to a new fire that consumed him, — the insatiable knowledge-hunger. "I suffer," he writes, "from a singular preoccupation, that of the rapidity and value of time. Doubtless it comes from having lost several years, and wishing to make them up. The aim that I fix for myself disappears as I approach it. It is a horizon which I fancy I can reach, but which enlarges and recedes at every step. I have proposed to make certain studies; to acquire certain kinds of knowledge, but it is like another voyage. You do not think of the ground gone over, it is the space yet to be travelled that absorbs your attention. We are never content with what we have, but always wishing for what we have not. That is especially true of knowledge, where the gaps seem to multiply in proportion as they are filled. *Ars longa, vita brevis.* Life is nothing more to me than a number of hours of which each one unemployed in a certain manner seems lost. And what a mournful echo this word 'lost' has in my mind. In this way, I always hear behind me the voice that says, 'Go on! go on!'"

In 1839, he took his degree of Bachelor of

Theology. He married. Public life might have begun for him, as an associate pastorate was offered him, but he refused it. He took a little country-house at Wangen, and there, in the perfect seclusion of a foreign country, gave himself up to further study. Some of his friends remonstrated with him on this course, declaring so much study unnecessary for the discharge of ministerial duties; but he protested that he could not conscientiously enter the pulpit with less, and that the truths he came into possession of must be the fruit of reflection and labor. His library became his world. During his attendance at the university, he had associated little with his professors and fellow-students, and now that he was wholly master of his time, he was not more inclined to squander it in the sterile intercourse of social gossip.

Indeed, something of the close student's reticence and coldness of manner clung to him all his life. Strangers found him exceedingly difficult to meet. He gave himself reluctantly, and even then not to everybody. His purity and refinement, his sincerity that refused to cloak its indifference, his preoccupation in the world of ideas, unfitted him for that free and easy

yet conciliatory intercourse that we call
neighborliness.   But those who were fortunate enough to awaken his interest and
regard, found in his friendship a life-long
possession and an exhaustless well of refreshing and delight.   He liked to meet his
friends alone, and never visited those whom
he particularly loved, but at such times as
he knew that he would meet no other visitor.

He is described to us as of slender build,
with a mobile, intellectual face well framed
by soft, abundant blonde hair; the forehead
high, the mouth delicate and expressive;
the eye cold, but capable of warming in the
fire of passion; and in his movements, gestures, looks, that indescribable air of authority and charm that belongs to superior
natures.

In 1844, the Neo-Calvinistic school,
founded at Geneva under the title of Free
School of Theology, offered Scherer a chair,
which he gladly accepted, thinking that he
had touched the aim of his life, little knowing that many and many a weary league still
lay between him and the real work that he
was destined to do.   The untiring research
did not end with the assumption of profes-
sorial duties.   Had it ended then, Edmond

Scherer might have quietly lived and died a college professor, honored in the narrow circle in which he moved, but wholly unknown to the literature of Europe. But the voice that had cried in his early youth, " Go on! Go on!" still urged him forward, and in 1851 began the revolution in him which he so vividly describes in the following passage : —

"The most profound revolution that can take place in the human mind is when the absolute escapes it, and with the absolute, the arrested outlines, the privileged sanctuary, and the oracles of truth. It is difficult to describe all the agitation of the heart, when we begin to recognize that our church and our system have not a monopoly of the good and the true; when we meet sincere and eminent men who profess the most opposed beliefs; when sin and justice become in our eyes the degrees of an infinite ladder that rises to the clouds and sinks into hell; when we discover that there is no error but has its mixture of truth, and no truth that is not partial, incomplete, and error-stained; when the relative appears to us like the absolute, and the absolute like an aim eternally pursued yet eternally inaccessible, and

4

truth like a mirror broken into a thousand fragments, all of which reflect the sky while no one reflects it wholly. Until then, submission was all that was necessary; now, examination becomes a duty. Authority and the absolute have disappeared at the same time, and since truth is nowhere concentrated within the hands of a single depository, it is a question, in future, of searching, proving, and selecting."

These profound revolutions in human life do not take place without some evidence of their existence, and Scherer's college-lectures began to betray the conflict in which he was engaged. When his friends reproved him for the boldness and newness of the ideas that crept into his lectures, he excused himself by saying that man does not learn what he wishes to learn, but learns without ceasing and in spite of himself what he *must* through the teachings of suffering and the course of events; that every new acquisition of knowledge necessarily modifies the whole mass of knowledge previously acquired, and that in this way take place the greatest spiritual revolutions, and that Christianity itself has acted on souls in no other way. He said that he had grown accustomed to distinguish between his tastes and reality, and that he felt the need of seeing things as they are, even when they were repugnant to his feelings or to his conscience. He said: "Logic knows no more characteristic example of fallacious argument than the following reasoning: I cannot explain this phenomenon, therefore, it is inexplicable: it is inexplicable, therefore, it ought to be referred to a direct intervention of the supreme power. The opposite conclusion ought to be drawn; every phenomenon has a cause, and until we know that cause we ought to suppose it natural."

From 1855 to 1859, he continued his lectures at Geneva, but in choosing his subjects, he carefully avoided anything of a doctrinal character, selecting from the New Testament such passages as are best suited to the development of the inner life, and sometimes confining himself to a simple study of texts. It was the beginning of the end; "the last effort," says his biographer, "of his theological science, and of a science in which his faith was no longer interested."

There was but one course open to an honest man who respects his intellect, and prefers its honor to its prostitution to worldly interests, and Scherer was an honest man. He prepared a careful, firm, and manly, yet modest report of his new attitude towards theology, and addressed this published report, entitled "La Critique et la Foi," to Dr. Merle D'Aubigné, president of the theological seminary of Geneva.

"I have not come to these views," he confesses in the report, "without much hesitation and effort. Doubt presented itself to my mind from the first day of my religious life. I have resisted it in every possible way. Many a time, I have voluntarily closed my eyes to the evidence of facts. I imitated that bad conservatism which believes that the edifice is menaced with ruin as soon as repairs are begun upon it."

Religion had been to Scherer a passion that had absorbed his whole heart, his whole range of feeling, but it had never been able to absorb wholly his large, penetrating, untiring intellect. The conflict between this passion and his reason consumed more than half the working years of life. He was forty-five when he freed himself from its bondage. He quitted Geneva never to return except as a traveller. Shortly after leaving Geneva, he gave away to different libraries and to his friends his large collection of theological works. He went to Strasburg for a time, and then settled permanently at Versailles.

In a note to one of his last articles on sociology, he sums up his intellectual experiences in this graphic way: "There are two classes of men among those consecrated by passion and earnestness. The one class have been awakened to the sentiment of duty. They have caught a glimpse of that pure and holy ideal of life which, once seen, takes complete possession of them; in Christian phraseology, they are converted, and then everything in them is conformed to this sublime vision. Their intellectual attitude is no longer that of research but that of defence of a possession. Their mind has become less inquiring and less exacting. They admit with secret complaisance the solutions favorable to their new conception of things. They choose to pass by all objections, and when these objections present themselves, they avoid looking them too closely in the face. They even go so far as to do a certain violence to their critical conscience; prejudiced in favor of a higher order of truths, they have lost their loyalty to the true. The convert has renounced science for faith. Such was my history at twenty.

"The second class of men have recognized the supreme authority of the true. They have said, in short, that all turns on a question of faith or of logic, of historic proof or of rational demonstration. They have not been able to convince themselves that truths, even of what is called faith or sentiment, can escape the necessity of being in harmony with the conditions of thought and fact. Where certainty seems impossible of attainment, they have learned to decline to give an opinion, and to remain in doubt. . . . The holy life and the beliefs upon which it rests, are not by that excluded or profaned. They preserve their beauty; they remain an ideal and a source of strength, but they can no longer claim a miraculous value. The scientific conception refers all things, if we may so express it, to natural history, and religion protests in vain; it has its place, like all the rest, in the science of nature. There is where I stood at forty."

The soul to which religion has once furnished the principles of a holy life cannot altogether escape, even in the quiet gladness of conscious growth and disillusionment, the passionate regret of what was once the light of life. It cannot learn to hate nor even to be indifferent to what it has so wholly loved. It cherishes an exquisite tenderness for what it renounces. Such was Scherer's attitude towards religion. There was nothing of the proselyting spirit in it. He could not profane what he had once so deeply loved, and he could be loyal, at least, to the memory of what it had once been to him. All light mockery of infidels was odious to him; even wit on such subjects hurt him as if it were a personal insult, and he would not even allow a smile in the discussion of subjects so sacred. "What is certain," says Sainte-Beuve, of Scherer in his criticism of the latter's "Mélanges d'histoire religieuse," "is that he is still and was always a Christian in this sense at least, that the Sermon on the Mount appears to him of divine inspiration, something after which humanity ought not to resemble humanity before it." Even after his published renunciations of Theology, Scherer's home remained a Christian home, and in it his wife preserved her faith intact. His attitude towards religion is admirably expressed in a comment to be found in his critical article on Sismondi. The comment is appended to his quotation of the following letter from Mme. Sismondi to her son:—

"It is not very surprising that we should incur the hatred of men in needlessly attacking the opinions on which their happiness is founded. These opinions may be erroneous, but long accepted errors are more respectable than those which we would like to substitute for them; for it is not the truth we find when we overthrow the system of religion that is generally adopted; because the truth, if it is not revealed, is hidden from the human mind in impenetrable shadows. Then, leave in peace the Trinity, the Virgin, and the Saints. To the majority of those who are attached to this doctrine, they are the columns that sustain the whole edifice; it will crumble to pieces if you shake them. And what would become of the souls whom you will have deprived of all consolation and hope? Piety is one of the sweetest affections of the soul, and that which is most necessary to its repose. We must have it in all religions except those in which, by force of pruning away the branches to which our senses cling, by force of spiritualizing, we fall into abstract ideas and a desolate vagueness." Scherer comments on this letter in the following manner: "That is beautiful! That is true! That is what we sometimes

need to repeat to ourselves, — all we who are
apt to confound so easily error with evil,
and to attack in souls that which makes their
strength, and more than that, their beauty.
Alas! blind pioneers working at the overthrow of the past, we know not what we do.
We yield to a power of which it seems sometimes as if we were the victims as well as
the instruments. The terrible dialectics
whose formulas we cipher, crushes us at the
same time that we crush others with it. It
is the future, undoubtedly, that we must
trust. Woe be to us, if we doubt it. And
yet, when the struggle ceases for a moment,
when the thinker becomes a man again,
when he sees the ruins that he has made,
and hears the groans he has extorted, — O,
how wild and rugged he finds his pathway
then; and how willingly he would give all
the pleasures of conquest for one of those
sweet flowers of piety and poetry that still
make fragrant the pathway of the humble."

Scherer was deeply convinced that the im-
prisonment of a spiritual idea in a dogma is
its death-blow. Change, implying adapta-
tion, growth, development, was for him the
law of the intellectual and moral life as well
as of physical life. He accuses his country-

men of a particular love of dogma manifested
in their inclination towards what is external.
"In everything," he writes, "we go from the
outside to the inside. We regulate all the
manifestations of human activity. We have
no confidence in the plastic force of life.
We think we can hold it in formulas, fix it
in our papers, produce it in our decrees.
Our institutions are not the expression of a
moral fact; they are a mould which we apply to society. They do not proceed from
our customs. They are an abstract product
of reason. Neither have we the taste nor
the understanding for liberty. In fact, liberty has no value, no meaning but to men
who have an inner law of action. We prefer the regular forms of mechanical movement to the free gait of spontaneity. The
inclination of which I speak, is betrayed in
religion as well as in public life. . . . We do
not understand religion unless it be reduced
to articles of faith. . . . It is high time we
were done with the superstition of dogma.
Dogma is not substance, it is shadow; it is
not living truth, it is dead truth. Humanity
does not live by abstract principles but by
great thoughts, and great thoughts come from
the soul. All thoughts that have ever borne

fruit among men have had their birth in the
mystic depths of our being, — in the spon-
taneous intuitions of our nature, in aspirations towards the infinite, in a thirst for the
beautiful and true, in sentiments of love and
justice. Great men are not those who rule
but those who inspire. They are not the
legislators, but the prophets. The words
that change the world are words of passion.
Later they cool; the lava stiffens. Then
comes formula. Recordings, creeds, char-
ters succeed to the free manifestations of the
Eternal Spirit. We wish to retain life by
fixing it and we end by stifling it.

"I know very well that it is impossible to
prevent the arrival of this hour of reflection,
that gives birth to dogma; but in the name
of heaven, let us not take shadow for substance; let us not extinguish the fire in order
to warm ourselves by its chilled cinders. . . .
It is impossible to imagine anything less dogmatic than Christianity in its origin. Christ
wrote nothing, decreed nothing, founded
nothing. He cast his word into the air as
the sower his seed, with the most sublime
confidence in the virtue of spiritual germs.
He teaches, but his teachings are not the
articles of a code or the propositions of a

catechism.   They are the cry of the soul to
God, and the cry of God to the soul.   He
brings   a   revelation,   and   this   revelation
teaches us quite simply to say: ' Our Father
which art in heaven.'   He changed the relations of men to one another, but he changed
them in exhorting us to do unto others what
we would that they should do unto us.   He
regenerated society.   He gave a new idea to
humanity.   He was the leader of an historical development; he transformed civilization, created a world, and all that by the
simple power of a soul that descended into
itself, into those luminous depths where it
found the pure image of man together with
the pure image of God.

" Catholicism is a development of Evangel-
ical Christianity, but a development which
is a decadence, and this decadence is precisely that which every idea suffers when it
passes from life to formula.   One must have
very little intuition of great things not to
feel to what degree the speculations of coun-
cils and the distinctions of scholasticism
detract from the majesty of the religion of
Christ. . . . It is the same with Protestant-
ism as with Catholicism.   In the beginning
with Luther, especially with the Luther of

the early years, him whom anabaptism had not yet intimidated, the Reformation is wholly a joyous soaring, a celestial confidence, enthusiastic deliverance, prophetic speech. Then come the confessions of faith, and after that, the dogmatic and the scholastic, until the theologians of the seventeenth century made of Protestant orthodoxy a skeleton as dry, as grimacing as ever was Catholic orthodoxy in the slumbers of the Middle Ages."

To Scherer, then, religion did not live in dogma, but in the passionate longing of the human heart for rest in faith, in something eternal, something infinitely purer and higher than itself, and in passionate effort to realize in its temporal life something of the beauty of the holiness it adores. It is in this sense that he writes: "It is complained that there is no longer any religion in the world; that the world of religion has disappeared; that the things of religion are dead. For my part, I do not believe it. Religion is like poetry; it always finds a place in which to strike its roots; it rises from its ashes; it will live as long as the human soul."

It is in this sense, too, that in renouncing

the claims of dogmatic theology, in rising to
the supreme heights of intellectual freedom,
Scherer still remained the most profoundly
religious man of his day. It was this well
of Puritan feeling in him that set him at
variance with his young contemporaries, and
made them complain of him that he judged
with his character and not with his intelligence. His ideal man was in no wise the
modern ideal. "His ideal," says Édouard
Rod, "is the honest man, in the old sense
of the expression; he, who according to La
Rochefoucauld piques himself on nothing,
and can be amorous as a madman but not as
a fool; he who according to La Bruyère
holds a medium between the clever man and
the good man; who acts simply, naturally,
without artifice, without a thousand singu-
larities, without pomp and without affectation; he of whom Chevalier de Meré said
that intelligence and honesty are above everything. If we try to complete these qualities by others that Scherer himself furnishes,
we shall find that the man has freed himself
from some of the laws that the moralists of
the old régime imposed upon him. He has
ceased to be satisfied with words; the philosophical seductions to which he has yielded,

have taught him certain things of which the
La Bruyères and La Rochefoucaulds were
ignorant; among other things, that there are
but 'facts and series of facts,' and that 'fact
is but the consciousness we have of it.' . . .
But the liberty, acquired in this high sphere
in which one rarely moves, does not prevent
him from remaining a gentleman in the practice of current life; a man of taste, re-reading more willingly than reading; loving
delicate and finished things; sensible to
force but more sensible still to perfection;
jealous of his liberty and too much alive to
distinctions to give way to violence, crudities, and brutalities; mindful of certain laws
of decorum which probably have no better
foundation than others, but which beautify
life; knowing that the absolute has no
authentic existence, but complying with its
laws as if he believed in it, — the honest
man of the eighteenth century completed
by what he is pleased to admit of the
nineteenth."

This ideal of which Rod says he would
despair of humanity if it were the definitive
and unchangeable type, seems to us infinitely preferable to that which he himself
sketches as the ideal man of the nineteenth

century. In learning just what that ideal is, according to Rod, we are better able to understand the intellectual and moral gap that separates Scherer from the majority of his young contemporaries. Rod begins by saying that the nineteenth century's ideal resembles Scherer's very little, but that he is not a blockhead for all that. "Without doubt he has lost definitively the faiths which serve as a law to the other; he knows it, and he has taken his stand; but in losing them, he has gained by freeing himself from all prejudice. The idea of the absolutely imperative escapes him, but he does not the less continue to do good from tradition, habit, and education. He no more believes in the absolute in æsthetics than in morals; but that does not prevent him from distinguishing enduring works from the temporary ones which he disdains. While knowing that the ideas which he has of the good and the beautiful are but relative, he holds none the less tenaciously to them, only he does not try to impose them on others; and applies himself to understanding even those manifestations of art that are the most remote from them. A philosopher having taught him that all error contains a portion of truth,

he has profited by this aphorism, whose consequences are numerous and of a character
that renders him very indulgent. Moreover,
truth and error are words that have no very
precise meaning to him, and he employs them
only with a mental reservation. His intellect
is developed at the expense of his character,
but it will soon teach him that character is
as indispensable as intelligence, and he will
make himself one of which he, only, will
know its artificial nature. One feature in
which he will differ greatly from his prede-
cessor is, that in art he will very likely prefer strength to delicacy, precisely because
strength is the quality most difficult for him
to obtain, and he will distrust perfection,
knowing too well how many faults it conceals, and that true masterpieces are never
perfect. Very eclectic in his tastes, he will
be able to like the corruption of Beaudelaire
without being corrupted, and will esteem M.
Zola in spite of his crudities. Do not think
that the reading of 'Fleurs du Mal' will
prevent him from enjoying the choruses of
'Athalie,' and be assured that even if Molière versifies badly, as Scherer has demon-
strated, he will always take pleasure in
hearing the 'Misanthrope;' as he is dispas-

sionate, he will be of easy commerce, and if
he holds the critic's pen, he will not use it
as a club against those who displease him
most; for he will always have sympathies
and antipäthies, — the intellect being able
to excuse everything, but not to make everything lovable.   This honest man whose complete portrait might fill many pages, is very
likely worth as much as the other.   He
would have irritated Edmond Scherer, who
has all his clear-sightedness, and has never
been able to console himself for having it."

We are greatly indebted to Rod for sum-
ming up in so unmistakable a manner, the
qualities that the modern Parisian school
think so admirable that they make them the
typical characteristics of the culture of the
nineteenth century.   It helps us to know
exactly what are the dangers that threaten
morality and real culture, for to adopt Rod's
own phraseology, we should despair of man-
kind were these qualities definitive and unchangeable; and we turn to Scherer's ideal
with a sense of love and respect that is
mingled with the deepest gratitude.   It is
good to feel in this man a character worthy
of all confidence because there is nothing
artificial in it.   It is not based on mere

"tradition, habit, or education;" it does not rest on something external. That which is its strength is part of itself; it proceeds from an instinctive love of purity and right as healthy and natural as the instinct that sets the cellar-plant to groping towards the light. Among the countless thousands who find it easier to adopt their opinions ready-made, here is a man whose opinions are a growth proceeding from his experiences, his broader contact with life. Here is a man who finds it more respectable to think even at the risk of thinking wrongly than not to think at all. There is a vast difference between living in your opinions and having your opinions live in you. In the first case you use your opinions as you do your house, for mere shelter and convenience. They are no more a part of you than your house and furnishings, and yet, like the latter, they may give you a certain prestige, a certain social status, but they are nothing that you can impart in living contact with your fellow men. They are not *in* you but *on* you. In the next case your opinions are a living part of your character. They give shape and consistency to it. They are felt in you as vitally active and reactive. You cannot sacrifice them without injury to yourself any more than you can lose an eye or an arm. If they change, it is by the slow, vital process of waste and assimilation. On the contrary, in the former case, you can change them as often as you can change your house, and with as little inconvenience or harm. This is the whole secret of that artificiality of which Rod boasts that the maker of his character alone knows how factitious it is.

It is good, too, to feel that Scherer recognizes that there *is* a distinction between right and wrong; that he does not blend black and white into a soft, acceptable gray, nor fall into sentimental pity or apotheosis of guilt. We are grateful to him for feeling the need to keep alive the old taste for the masterpieces of sound literature; the joy in a noble sentiment nobly expressed. We are grateful for his love of truth so faithful and austere that no fad, no fashion, no clamor of the hour can turn him from her, — grateful that he could love her so well that when in ignorance or blindness he had worshipped her under some mistaken form, he could quit the false, and champion the true with no cowardly fear of being ridiculed for vacillation or of being passed by on the other side and left to faint and perish by the wayside. This man can take no joy in corruption that he knows corrupt. He cannot find the perfumes of Arabia in the stenches of gutters and cloacas, and when he holds the pen of the critic, he will use it in the interests of moral cleanliness and moral health.

This is the work that Edmond Scherer has found to do, and it is a work to which he comes in the maturity of his powers after much travail of spirit and deep, wide, ardent, unremitting study. During the latter years of his stay in Geneva, when his interest in theological questions began to decline, he had taken up the study of Italian. English he had learned at Monmouth, and German at Strasburg. Therefore he had free access to the leading literatures of Europe in their own language, and no critic since Sainte-Beuve has been so well informed. He began his critical work on his removal to Versailles. A study of Hegel in the October number of the " Revue des deux Mondes," 1860, was his début in journalism. "No labor frightened him," says his biographer; "he was capable of shutting himself up for months in the meditation of a subject. . . . He was hardly ever seen on the railroad be-

tween Paris and Versailles without a book
and a pencil in his hand, and it was not for
everybody that he would make the sacrifice
of putting his book into his pocket."

In the late Franco-Prussian war, while
the Prussians occupied Versailles, Scherer
addressed a correspondence in English to the
"Boston Review." He preferred English
literature to that of any other foreign nation,
and has left a volume of articles on the leading English writers. These criticisms, however, are not in his best vein. In spite of
all his cosmopolitan experiences and learning, the classical French taste for clearness,
chastity of style, and directness of statement, was particularly strong in him, and
faults of expression, eccentricities, or affectations sometimes rendered him insensible
to vigor of thought. He himself writes to
be intelligible; he has, he says, no taste for
clouds. In his notice of Guizot's "Mé-
moires," he writes: "I have a horror of
Carlyle's books. I prefer a hundred times
the dull manner of our compatriot to the
brazen affectations of the Scotch humorist."
Ruskin, too, he accuses of affectation of
depth, and a laborious search for expression.
Matthew Arnold's clearness attracts him

strongly. He calls Arnold the apostle of
intellectual civilization; the liveliest, most
delicate, most elegant of critics; the critic
who has been most fertile in ideas to which
he has given the most piquant expression;
and declares it a rest to open one of Arnold's
books after reading those great mannerists,
Ruskin and Carlyle, "of whom our neighbors are so wrongly proud."

All displays of rhetoric offended him.
He says that Taine makes him think of a
wooden doll with steel springs. Of the
rhetoric of Comte de Lisle, he writes: "I
do not know why, but I never meet these
studied efforts in style without feeling a little ashamed for the author. He took so
much trouble to write finely, and he has so
rarely succeeded." He thought that the
best proof that the sermon is a false species
of literature, "is the rhetoric to which it is
condemned. Manner that goes beyond matter; expression destined not to render, but
to simulate emotion; the need of convincing
one's self by straining the voice, heating
one's self, gesticulating violently; emotion
by emphasis, — this is what we mean by
rhetoric. There is a well-known saying,
'You are angry, therefore you are in the

wrong,' which with a slight modification I should like to apply to preachers: 'You declaim, therefore you are in a false position.'"

He touches finely the note of falsity in Chateaubriand, whom he calls the man of phrase and effect. "Chateaubriand's manner has the seal of literature in decadence, — disproportion between depth and form. There is a letter from him to Joubert in which he recounts a voyage. It was night. 'A tiny end of a crescent moon,' he says, 'was in the sky just on purpose to prevent me from lying, for I feel sure that if the moon had not been there, I should have put it into my letter, and it would have been just like you to convince me of falsehood, with your almanac in your hand.'"

It would have been like Scherer, too. He had a fine, manly directness of statement, — a clear, unwavering consciousness of the value of the fact behind the expression, and he would not alter his fact an iota for the sake of making the expression more brilliant or more captivating. "Taste," he writes, "conceals the labor it costs, and to-day, we want the proceeding to show itself. Taste is delicacy, and we appreciate nothing but force. It is moderation, and we applaud precisely what is immoderate. Formerly, the pencil was never light enough; now, it must pierce the paper. Tints ought to be harmonious; now, they must be striking. Expression no longer addresses itself to the mind but to the senses. . . . Formerly, a writer did not speak till he had something to say. Romanticism, which has taught us to prefer force to moderation, has also taught us to subordinate matter to manner. The famous principle 'art for art's sake' is understood in the sense that sounds and images have a value in themselves. . . . The writer is no longer a thinker but a virtuoso. He no longer needs sense, knowledge, intellect, passion, humor; only one thing is demanded of him, — *chic*."

Scherer declares that the "great intellectual virtues are the curiosity that states problems, the sincerity that studies them, and the courage that does not recoil from the solutions," and he himself has these virtues. His strength as a critic lies in his absorbing interest in human individuality and his consequent search for the writer behind his works. "However real the pleasure that I have always felt in the commerce of letters," he writes, "I think that even in works

of imagination and in poetry, my principal
interest has been awakened by the person of
the author." With this end in view of understanding and enjoying the author, he
makes a virtue of curiosity. Nothing is
indifferent to him that can illustrate character, nothing too trivial for suppression, and
he confesses that he would give all the phil-
osophies of art and history for some simple
literary chats or anecdotes, a volume of Bos-
well or of Saint-Simon. He has a wonderful selective power, — the power that he
praises in another of putting his finger on
the characteristic trait of men and things.
He does not go round and round a subject;
he goes straight to its centre. Hence his
power to draw admirably a literary portrait.
He has exquisite delicacy, the refinement
that can appreciate refinement; and some of
these portraits not only elucidate the characters of certain authors, but enrich criticism
by furnishing valuable psychological analyses of those mental peculiarities that result
in certain forms of morbid literature. Among
the finest of these portraits is that of Maurice de Guérin. In the course of his article
on the unfortunate young poet and journalist, Scherer says: "Melancholy is the prod-

uct of an advanced civilization. The forces
of nature are at last subdued; the struggle
of man with man is finished or arrested; toil
and war are replaced by abundance, luxury,
and peace. The satiety that follows possession; literature, art, and science giving
a more energetic development to mental
forces; the mind pushing forward to the
ultimate limits of all things, — such are the
causes of those solitary griefs with which
epochs of combat and victory are unac-
quainted. When man gives himself wholly
up to the interests of external life, his
thought is simple. It grows richer, more
complex, and more troublesome when he begins to descend into himself. A thousand
new questions arise; another world to be
conquered opens before him. In its modern
form, melancholy finds its first expression in
Rousseau. Rousseau is its ancestor, I was
about to say its founder; and what a singular
rôle, when we come to think of it, this extraordinary genius plays in universal initia-
tives! His influence separates into two
parts the history of the eighteenth century.
The ' Contrat social ' dominates the French
Revolution: ' Héloïse ' inaugurated the reign
of paradox. Rousseau is the father of vir-

tuous and super-sensitive souls : he taught
humanity a new sentiment, that of the
beauty of nature.   In short, he was the first
man to give to the world the spectacle of a
soul looking inward to observe how it lives,
nourishing itself on its sorrows, feeding itself on its own substance.

"The influence of Rousseau as the father
of modern melancholy did not at once make
itself completely felt.   The struggles of the
Revolution and the wars of the Empire were
not favorable to reveries.   'René,' it is
true, appeared in 1802, and 'Obermann' did
not spring up and bear fruit until twenty
years later in the full Restoration.   The
great shocks and frightful crises were succeeded by moral exhaustion.   Men's souls
were wearied of everything, even of hope.
M. de Lamartine gave the tone to our literature.   Poetry, dramas, and novels became
subjective.   'Consolations,' 'Impressions,'
'Inner Voices,' — these titles mark the prevailing key.   Such was the medium in which
Maurice de Guérin was born and lived.

"Melancholy, moreover, invests itself with
various forms.   René is not like Obermann;
René is dominated by passion.   Life for him
is concentrated in love.   'O God,' he cries,

in the midst of his profoundest grief, ' if
you had but given me a woman after the desires of my heart!' Add to that the artist
who seeks an effect, the poet who poses before himself, a vanity that puts a sting into
every feeling, even tenderness, and you will
have Chateaubriand, and in him you will
have René.

"Obermann, on the other hand, is saddened by reflection. He has suffered an
irreparable loss, that of desires.

"Maurice de Guérin has also his peculiar
sorrow. In reading him, we sometimes
fancy that we are listening to Obermann,
but to a more eloquent Obermann, one with
a finer mastery of the art of expression.
And yet the root of sadness is not quite the
same in these two melancholy men. Maurice is especially haunted by the idea of his
powerlessness; he is paralyzed by what he
calls his inner wretchedness. He does not
feel himself fitted for the struggle of life;
he is worn out with alternate soaring and
sinking; his melancholy is that of discour-
agement. Besides, Maurice is an invalid;
he is frail, consumptive; he will die at
twenty-nine. Perhaps, if we could get to
the bottom of melancholy we should always

find some such want of equilibrium of faculties and, as a final cause, some organic decay. The melancholy man is an incomplete being, attacked in the sources of life, — a man who will breathe out eloquent complaints, but who will scarcely reach finished art.

"The true artist, he who dominates nature and man, who reproduces them in an impersonal conception, — a Shakespeare, a Goethe, a Walter Scott, — these are sound men. They do not know what it is to feel their pulse. Their peace of mind is not at the mercy of the weather. They look at life with serenity. If there is one thing that they do not understand in the infinite variety of human nature which it is their business to depict, it is, very likely, just this solitary, subjective wretchedness of weaker beings. Melancholy is the product of an organization nervous, impressionable, acute, exquisite, but incompatible with the harmony of forces and the elasticity of a robust temperament.

"The want of equilibrium among the faculties is betrayed in Maurice, by a disproportion between his intelligence and his will. He is all thought. Action and moral life are wanting. He has only desires, nay, less than that, only feeble wishes. Seated at the crossing of a thousand roads, he does not know which to take. His strength is consumed in irresolution. He is the prey of a secret contradiction in his nature. He conceives grand things and he loves them. He catches a glimpse of fame and he is enamoured of it. He is touched at the name of heroism and virtue. No one has a higher ideal, and it is from this height that he falls back upon himself, upon the weakness of his character and the timidity of his will. His nature contracts and dilates in turn. His life is a continual alternation of buoyancy and exhaustion, of ambitious dreams and heart-breaking deceptions. He would like to be guided; he would like to yield to others the decisions that he cannot make, and he cannot even do that. On whatever side he looks, he sees but attempts without results, abortive creations, convulsive efforts which resemble, he himself says, the incoherent words of a madman.

"More thought than will, but that is not all; more thought than reason. Maurice has no taste for the mechanical operations of the intellect. He cares neither for logic

nor systems. By so much as he excels in
the analysis of sensations, by just so much
is he a stranger to that of ideas. His world
is the subjective one. He descends therein
as a miner into the bowels of the earth. He
applies a microscope to it, like a naturalist
in the pursuit of the ultimate phenomena of
life. He watches himself suffer; he observes himself watch. Yet this subtle and
unlimited analysis in which M. de Guérin
takes pleasure, is united in him with great
activity of the imagination, and we see two
faculties that apparently ought to exclude
each other, on the contrary, mutually aid
and excite each other. This apparent contradiction existing between minute sorrowful observation and an active ardent
imagination is another feature of the melancholy temperament.

"Look at these suffering geniuses: they
live absorbed in themselves, and yet they
love to plunge into the contemplation of
nature. Association with men wounds and
depresses them. The going and coming of
so many busy people irritates them. They
feel themselves inferior to these people, so
far as the conduct of life is concerned, and
at the same time superior with all the supe-

riority of a human being who thinks of another who has never known self-reflection. Hence a mute, concentrated rancor which is appeased in solitude, especially in the presence of the grand scenes of nature. Not that melancholy is forgotten there. If the melancholy man abandons himself to Nature, if he identifies himself with her, it is only to lend her his own preoccupations. The ceaseless change of all things, the life of beings, the succession of generations, the law of suffering, the responsibility of the universal order, — all that is still we ourselves; it is the very mystery of our destiny, and in contemplating this vast current of life in which individual existence seems but a shallow ripple on the surface of the water, in plunging by thought into the infinite in presence of which the finite is but a transitory form, we lose ourselves only to find ourselves again. We are conscious of our infinite littleness; and is not the sovereign act of personality to know ourselves in the plenitude of our vanity? Hence the double effect of contemplation on the reflective mind. It calms it and troubles it: it is its joy, because it wrests man from the cares of life, the miseries of society, the dis-

tractions of activity, to lead him back to the
fundamental unity; but at the same time
it feeds his melancholy, because it brings
vividly before his eyes again the mirage
of universal illusion. It must be acknowledged, however, that this development of
the contemplative faculties of the mind is
not accomplished except to the detriment
of intellectual vigor and even of energy of
feeling. . . .

"Maurice de Guérin has given us some
beautiful pages, but he has very especially
left us an example. There are two ways of
consoling ourselves in life: one is by that
wisdom which, in admitting the sovereign
right of whatever is, takes away the sting of
evil; the other is by that art which, in
transforming subjective emotion, in reducing
it to measure and harmony, in freeing from
it the poetical and ideal element, obliges
the soul to withdraw from the circle of sensations to live a broader and healthier life.
It is into this road that Maurice de Guérin
was about to enter when premature death
carried him away."

In this analysis, Scherer recognizes a fact
that is only beginning to be generally admitted in literary criticism, but which as

surely has its proper place there as the law
of gravitation has its place in physics. This
fact is that temperament, organic well-being
or ill-being, in a great measure determine the
form and character of thought, and hence the
form and character of literature. Scherer
notes this fact again in his review of the
French critic Alexandre Vinet.

"Vinet," he says, "like all writers, has
the style of his temperament. He was in
feeble health. An infirmity contracted at
the age of twenty made a martyr of him for
the rest of his life. He was frail, delicate,
nervous, without sap or gayety. He knew
nothing of the body but its burden and
suffering. Nothing could be more sensitive and less sensual than his nature. His
only pleasures were those of the intellect.
Driven back upon himself by timidity and
ill-health, he had learned to live in an inner
world. . . . He was the most profound and ingenious writer we know, but his thought had
not substance enough, nor his style enough
of color. He had gone out of the tradi-
tional school of French literature which he
admired, however, more than anybody, and
which demands, before all else, clearness,
and loves simple lines and large masses. In

this respect Vinet was like Joubert; he also, ill, fastidious, saying exquisite things with a thread of a voice, understanding everything, and creating nothing. Both of distinguished nature, but whose distinction depends upon temperament and the very absence of vigor, — nature I should say of the critic. The true artist has health. Shakespeare, Bossuet, Walter Scott, are men who were well; as for Joubert and Vinet, they wrote in bed, supported by a pillow, covering little sheets of paper with fine handwriting. Now, the public, in general, is in good health. It does not understand invalids and does not like them."

It may be added, here, that if the public is not in good health, or weak enough to be influenced by those who are not, it is apt to turn to what is morbid in literature and to ignore or underrate what is sound. In such crises it is more than ever the duty of the faithful critic to brave the caprices and the hysterical anger of the weak or invalid public, in the interests not only of art and literature, but of moral health. It was Scherer's lot to wield the critic's pen during one of these crises in France, — the period of Zola, Baudelaire, and the ultra-realists, — and he wielded it faithfully.

"I am inclined to believe," he says, "that a poet, in the highest sense of the word, cannot be a corrupt or frivolous man. The very cultivation of art, this direction of the mind, this ideal turn of thought implies a sort of moral life. The conception of the beautiful is something pure, and all impurity is an attack upon the æsthetic perfection of a work. The great poet is healthy."

Scherer recognizes clearly that it is easy to excite curiosity, especially by the treatment of unusual subjects in unbridled language. Therefore Zola's thousands of readers and dozens of editions do not disconcert him in the least. He says: "An author's merit is not a question of the number of his readers, but of who the readers are, whether they will re-read him, and how long he will remain in favor. To excite curiosity is one thing; to excite interest is another. The difficulty is not in finding a public, but in satisfying the true public whose opinion counts and whose judgment lasts. The fate of literary works depends upon a few persons who do not read from idleness, curiosity, love of novelty, or love of scandal, but who read as thinkers and artists, with attention and reflection, applying to the book they

hold before them an understanding exercised
by habitual association with the masterpieces
of the human mind.   These are the readers
whom Zola does not interest because he conducts them to a society to which they willingly remain strangers.   Whatever talent a
novelist may have, he will never give me
pleasure by introducing me in his books to
men who may be my fellow-creatures, but
with whom I have nothing in common, either
in manner of life, tastes, or language.   One
may be democratic by principle or by resignation, a great partisan of the equal rights
of citizens; he may even work for his part,
in breaking down more and more the distinctions of class and rank, but that does not
prevent him from preferring to live among
his own.   I may be a philanthropist, and feel
a sincere sympathy for suffering creatures, a
true pity even for the vicious and the criminal; but these honorable sentiments do not
make me find pleasure in the description of
a beggar's hole or of a mason's drunkenness.
. . . It is not enough. that an object be depicted with fidelity to please us; it is not
enough that a description be exact in order
to interest.   What matters acuteness of observation, or even the power with which an

object is reproduced, if the object itself has no attraction? Whom does Zola think to please when he employs twenty or thirty pages in describing the cabbages, lettuce, and carrots heaped on a market-pavement, and the various preparations from pork in a butcher's shop? M. Zola thinks we ought to learn to tell whether or not the blood-pudding will be good. 'Look! this is the best sign. The blood is dripping and I catch it, beating it with my hand in the bucket. It must be good and hot, creamy, without being too thick. . . . I beat, beat, see?' continued the boy, making gestures in the air as if he were whipping cream. 'Well, when I take out my hand and look at it, it must look as if it were greased with blood in such a way that the red glove will be of the same red in every part. Then you can't make a mistake in saying, the pudding will be good.'

"There is a lesson that evidently does the greatest honor to M. Zola's knowledge as a specialist; only I should like to know who the readers are that such a description can charm, if they are not the workmen themselves whose labors are so knowingly described. But in the name of what principle

of art do you inflict upon me, who am not a
pork-butcher, so vulgar, not to say so revolting, a reality?   I do not want to see this
bucket into which you plunge your arm with
such delight; and this page of which you are
so proud only inspires me with disgust. . . .
It is said that Louis XIV. liked the odor of a
water-closet.   Zola, too, likes a stench.   Nobody thinks of disputing his pleasures with
him, only we should like a little toleration
for those who have noses that are made differently from his. . . . Some subjects charm
him that are disagreeable or repugnant to
other people.   Baudelaire was of this school
of æsthetics *à rebours*.

" 'Les charmes de l'horreur n'enivrent
que les forts.' Zola has adopted this maxim,
save that he substitutes the dirty for the
horrible.   His ideal in literature is the
'human beast' set entirely free.   Now, we
know how agreeable this beast is when set
at liberty.   Let M. Zola take pleasure, if he
likes, in the discoveries to which his predilection conducts him, — the lowest depths
of bestiality, — that is his business.   Let
him create, and at the same time satisfy his
morbid appetite in cultivating this kind of
literature.   The friends of good sense, good

taste, and good morals may pity him and complain of him, but, after all, he has his personal rights. The only thing we ask of him is not to overwhelm with his ferocious contempt the man who happens to have the prejudices of reason and decency.

"I do not think that there is anything of the prude in me. One of my favorite readings is that very Shakespeare of whom Zola says, sillily enough, that his drama is the triumph of the 'human beast.' The fact is, I could overlook much of Zola's shamelessness if he had a little of the depth of poetry or even of the humor and *verve* of the master whom he invokes. Is it my fault that he produces on me the effect of those impressionists, as they are called, who think that, in order to become artists, they must leave drawing and perspective out of painting? In literature, Zola has suppressed substance and form, thought and talent. I see in him no observation except of things material and external; and as for his style, it seems to me to be absolutely lacking in charm and piquancy. He seems to write with the point of a horn on leaves of lead. There is no style but where there is somebody holding the pen, and something worth the saying. The reader must find himself in the presence of an intelligence, a soul, a temperament, if you like, at any rate, of real human nature. He must come in contact with a true individuality; he must come under the charm or feel the grip. Zola has neither drawing, color, relief nor movement. It goes without saying that we do not ask distinction and poetry of him, because he professes contempt for these things. But we never find in him what can do no harm to any prose, — the happy expression, vivacity, wit, imagination. In him everything is dull without being either just or appropriate. . . .

"The attractions which the 'human beast' has for Zola are so pronounced that a predilection for the turpitudes of society becomes in his eyes the standard of value in a writer. Appearing to have a wide knowledge of foreign languages and literatures, he informs us that the drama and the novel are no longer to be found in England or Germany. And why? Because in these countries public opinion does not allow a description of the 'ulcers that consume humanity.' According to Zola, literature will be pathological, or it will not exist at all. Dickens finds grudging favor with our critic.

He grants him penetrating emotion, intense life; but it is plain to see for what he reproaches him; — women can read Dickens, and confess that they have read him."

Scherer is no less severe on Baudelaire and his school. He says: "There are writers who possess certain gifts without being artists, who have a certain talent without being able to compose a work. But Baudelaire has nothing; neither heart, intelligence, language, reason, fancy, enthusiasm, not even the art of composition. He is grotesque from impotence. His only title to glory is in having contributed to create an æsthetics of debauchery, the poem of the brothel. He has rotted, body and soul, and in a state of complete exhaustion, he puts into verse this refuse of himself. He feels dirty and he is proud of it. He affects an attitude, exposes his ulcers as a warrior his honorable wounds.

> ' Nous avons, nations corrompues,
>   Aux peuples anciens des beautés inconnues,
>   Des visages rongés par les chancres du cœur.'

Or he plays the misanthrope, then pities himself for his abject state, or tries to dignify the platitudes of venal love with a savor of pessimistic bitterness: 'O Satan, prends pitié de ma longue misère.'

"Fortunate for him were there some trace of real feeling beneath these affectations, a remnant of sincere humanity beneath these attitudes, the blossoming of some flower on this dunghill! But, no, nothing but the Bohemian who imagines himself a nobleman; nothing but license and shamelessness fancying itself strength. And this silliness and affectation, this barefaced licentiousness are as wearisome as they are impure.

"Baudelaire, who has become the head of a school of writers, has his ancestors. A man is always the son and grandson of somebody, only in this case, instead of weakening, the racial characteristics have gone on accentuating with every generation. Byron's pose is that of misanthropical dandyism. He only attains to disorder and libertinism. In Alfred de Musset the pose becomes display, the libertinism vice. Debauchery begins to call itself by its own name, to consider itself genteel, and to take the place formerly occupied by sentiment or passion. The line bends with Théophile Gautier. Gautier poses, but in another way, as 'the child of the century,' — as an Olympian. He is more immoral than Musset, but in another manner, — immoral like nature, simply a stranger to the distinction between good and evil. With Baudelaire the line takes another bend; depravity is regarded as morality, and cynicism turns into boastfulness. This is the dictum of Paul Bourget himself.

"Are we at the end? No. The end of this road is never reached, and that is its condemnation. 'Les Fleurs du Mal'! Why flowers? Why not the crude evil itself? Poetry! Why poetry? Art! — why not reality, and by preference the most repugnant reality? Enough of sheep-folds! Give us pigsties! It is said that M. Zola has made disciples who have in turn relegated him to a place among the Berquins.[1] Parliament ought to restrict by law the license of obscenity. It is true that obscenity has its defenders, but men who have wives and daughters are in the majority.

"I have always said that literature once stung by the horsefly of lechery is condemned to go to the very end, that is to say, to the point where the last remnants of modesty in the most debauched civilization finish by revolting.

[1] Berquin, a writer of the eighteenth century, the first creator of child's literature as it exists to-day.

"The Baudelaireists invoke precedents, quote authorities, — Regnier, Rabelais. Let us come to an understanding, once for all, on this subject of Rabelais. Do you like him equally well in every part? Do you like him *in spite* of or *because* of? Do you walk on tiptoe through the sewers, or do you wallow there in delight? If such are your tastes, well and good; there is nothing to be said. As for Regnier, I am like Boileau. I cannot admire his bedraggling the muses with Macette.[1] But what a singular effect all this passage from Boileau to which I allude, produces on the reader of the present day! He speaks there of the 'chaste reader' and of 'modest ears.' He seems to think that the French reader wishes to be respected. To judge from the authors of our time, we might be tempted to believe that French readers wish to be treated like old blackguards.

"The Baudelaireists declare that genius and talent have their privilege, their magic that excuses everything. I deny with the most perfect conviction that a poem can be made out of debauchery. There are books

[1] Macette, a hypocritically devout old courtesan in Regnier's poem of the same name.

and brilliant poems that have the worm of
rottenness at bottom, but how can any one
be blind to the fact that they belong to literature but in proportion to what there is of
soundness in them? A man may have dirty
hands and do beautiful work, but the beautiful work is not made with the dirt. At any
rate, it is by no means Baudelaire who can
prove that it is so made. No reputation is
so utterly unwarranted as that of 'Fleurs
du Mal.' In the absence of sentiment and
ideas, of inspiration and *verve*, not even the
technical skill of a Théophile Gautier is to
be found. It is a painful and fatiguing ham-
mering; a crowd of metaphors whose falsity
makes them appear burlesques; a confusion
of expressions whose impropriety resembles
a parody. His images are never either true
or beautiful; night is a 'partition,' the sky
a 'lid.' There are some passages so laugh-
ably absurd that they seem to have been produced in a wager. Baudelaire's only merit
and only strength is that he has had the
courage of his vice. But it seems that that
is exactly what makes his attraction. Es-
quimaux, too, we are told, like only rotten
fish.

"Do not be surprised at the heat with which

I attack certain tendencies in contemporaneous literature. It would be too cruel to believe that their degradation represents the
actual state of society in France. Good
God!—how far we are from the 'honest
man' of the eighteenth century, alas! and
even from the 'gentleman' of fifty years ago.
I can conceive of a democratic literature,
strong and incorrect, without taste but not
without sap, but I refuse to admit that art
cannot become democratic without becoming
bestial. And at the same time I can conceive of a literature refined, aristocratic, if
you like to term it such, searching new
paths according to a constant law of literature, but I can never bring myself to regard
Baudelaire and Baudelaireism as a legitimate
form of this research. Baudelaireism is not
the literature of a society destined to live.
It is a literature of—I dare not write the
word, you will find it in the prologue to ' Gar-
gantua.' I shall content myself with saying
that it is the literature of a generation with
vitiated blood and ruined constitution."

At the death of Sainte-Beuve in 1869,
Scherer succeeded to his critical authority.
Two men were probably never more unlike
in certain respects than these two great rep-

resentatives of French criticism. The one
with a truly Protean power of transforma-
tion, enabling him to understand all forms
of thought and modes of expression, no matter how widely divergent; the other never
being quite able to divest himself of a certain austerity of sentiment and exquisite perfection of taste that resulted in limitations
in one direction, but rendered him especially sensitive to the most delicate charms
of literature. The one erring in judgment
sometimes through over-sympathy with the
coarser experiences of life, — a man of the
world, skilled in the use of circumlocutions
in calling the false and the puerile by their
proper names; the other a man whom society cannot intimidate nor make indulgent,
and who will say what he means in incisive
and unmistakable language. But both men
have this in common: both are intensely interested in human individuality. To both,
the author is as much, if not more, than his
writings. Each, therefore, finds enjoyment
in the critical work of the other, and has
paid his tribute to the ability that produced
him that enjoyment. Writing of Sainte-
Beuve, Scherer says: —

"The world is the subject of our creations

and our judgments. To live, to see, to feel, `
to open one's mind to all things, one's soul
to all impressions, — that is the secret of art
and knowledge. Not, however, that the artist and the critic study the world in the
same way. The first acts as a master. He
commands the world he observes; he sees it
as he makes it; he impresses the stamp of
his genius upon it. The true critic is more
impersonal; he knows how to withdraw from
himself and some of his mental peculiarities.
He tries to see every object in its own character.   He identifies himself in turn with
all that is offered to him.   In order better
to penetrate the essence of things, he abandons himself to them and is transformed
into their semblance. To understand is to
go out of one's self in order to be transported as far as possible into the bosom of
realities.   It is to receive their impression;
it is to participate their life. Now, does
not criticism consist especially in understanding everything?

"M. Sainte-Beuve understands everything,
because he has tried everything, felt everything; he has not only tried everything and
felt everything, but he has been completely
transformed every time. He has passed suc-

cessively through several existences. M.
Sainte-Beuve has been philosopher, Saint-
Simonian and Catholic; he has been ascetic
and man of the world. He has had his political fever and recovered from it. He has
written to the 'Globe,' the 'National,' the
'Constitutionnel.' He has written poetry;
he has composed a novel, a history, portraits.
He has been one of the frequenters of a romantic *cénacle*, and has gone farther than
any one in adoration of the gods to whom
incense was burned there, and he has broken
the idols that he adored. . . .

"We have recognized in M. Sainte-Beuve
one of the princes of criticism. What does
that mean, and what must we think of the
line of work in which he excelled? The
importance of criticism may appear exaggerated, at present. Its rôle, however, represents a need of our age. Besides, criticism
has changed very much. We wish it now
to explain things, facts, man himself. Criticism is no longer a simple reflection on
works of the mind. It has become one of
the instruments, or, if you like, one of the
applications, of modern science. Thus it
tends daily to enlarge its sphere. We have
seen how it has been transformed under the

hands of M. Villemain and M. Sainte-Beuve.
It will not stop there. Nothing strikes the
attentive man more than the continual enlargement of the scientific horizon, the up-
lifting, if I may so speak, of the intellectual
soil, and as a consequence, the incessant dis-
placement of the point of view. It is a revolution of which a new phase is daily passing
under our eyes. Yet we do not discern it
except on the condition of isolating ourselves
for the moment, and taking a standpoint in
the past. We can already foresee the moment in which present criticism with all its
marvellous aptitudes will in its turn become
insufficient; in which we shall demand from
the critic more positive knowledge, more
familiarity with natural science, with history, religion, criticism, and the great philosophical speculations.

"It is nevertheless true that the interest of
all researches remains concentrated on man
and society, that is to say, on ourselves.
This is the point to which our thoughts incessantly return, and this is what assures a
permanent attraction to the works of Sainte-
Beuve. He has represented to us under
many diverse aspects this object of our perpetual study. He has added to our knowl-

edge of human nature. He has shown himself to be a faithful and sincere painter. He has not been, to use his own expression, the advocate of a single cause, but the inexorable observer. His conception of things might be more elevated, but would it be so true? His manner of considering life might be more heroic, but at the same time would it not risk being narrower? I am not insensible, by any means, to the nobleness of grand resolutions, to the dramatic interest of the moral struggle, to the spectacle of the man who, alone on his rock, opposes to nature and destiny the inflexible energy of a principle. . . . Who is not touched by the grandeur of Pascal, by his abnegation, his poverty, his hair-cloth, the disease so wholly accepted, so complete a detachment from the most legitimate feelings; but who does not tremble even while admiring? Who does not see that if all this is beautiful, it is at the same time forced and excessive? Who does not stifle in so cramped a place? Who does not recognize that the world seen thus from the garret-windows of a cloister, is not, after all, the real world such as God has made it? Pascal solves the problem by simplifying the terms and eliminating some of the factors.

"There is an age, I know, in which we love to take questions in this way, by their absolute side, — to retrench them by some sublime act of the will.   Later, we learn to dread this simplicity as a snare.   We have felt the power of the insensible demonstration of a simple contact with reality.   We are athirst to know the universe as it is, in all its fulness and complexity, and then we are disposed to pardon a great deal to a writer like Sainte-Beuve, who shows himself simple, sincere, and who reproduces in his pages something of the infinite variety, if also something of the imperturbable equanimity, of nature."

A review of "Endymion" gives Scherer an admirable opportunity to bring into relief two characters so opposite and so individual as those of Gladstone and Lord Beaconsfield.

"Gladstone's," he says, "is essentially a moral nature.   The categories to which he refers all things are those of good and evil. Yet this great seriousness that excludes extravagance does not exclude enthusiasm. Mr. Gladstone brings the fervor of faith into all the causes that he espouses.   He is essentially a believer.   There are noble sides to his character, — sincerity, justice, ardor, —

but there are also some defects in it. His
gravity lacks humor; his solidity becomes
stiffness. His intellect, endowed with the
most varied aptitudes, served by a prodigious
power of work and prodigious activity, able
to descend from the general direction of an
empire to the technical details of a bill or
the complicated accounts of a budget, — his
intellect is more extended than flexible. His
reasonings are abstract, because they are more
preoccupied with principles than with realities. His judgments are absolute, because
they elevate every truth to the same standard of value, — that of an article of religion.
This explains Gladstone's tendency to become more and more radical every day;
radicalism being nothing else than the application of the absolute to politics. Unfortunately, politics is precisely the most
relative thing in the world; so that radicalism is serviceable only in the production of
revolutions, and in ordinary times perpetually risks setting institutions in advance of
customs.

"What Gladstone is in public affairs, so is
he in his books. Solidity, sincerity are interpreted by conscientious study and exactness of. erudition; but at the same time the

absence of suppleness and acuteness are betrayed by the weakness of his criticism.
Mr. Gladstone, with his need of ready-
made theses, carries his mental submission
into the study of the Iliad as into the study
of the Bible. He no more doubts Homer and
the siege of Troy than Moses and the crossing of the Red Sea. He is even pleased to
unite the two subjects into a single faith and
to make of Homeric mythology an echo of
Christian revelation. Mr. Gladstone, in
fact, is a survivor of scholasticism. He
still belongs to those centuries of human
thought in which intellectual force is ap-
plied to the ideas furnished by tradition, in
which no one dreams of disputing, and in
which the acutest subtlety is accompanied by
the most superstitious respect for authority.

"Take the contrary of Mr. Gladstone in
every respect, and you will have Lord Beaconsfield's character. In him the keynote
is scepticism. He believes in success and
that nothing succeeds like it. In consequence, he is not disposed to regard morality too closely in his manner of arriving at
success. He has less worth than his rival,
but he has more ingenuity; less austerity,
but more geniality; less depth, but more

worldliness. Very inferior in the study of
details, he has not less courage when it is a
question of a resolution to be taken, especially if this resolution involves something
adventurous. I dare not say that Lord Beaconsfield is the more clever of the two in his
management of men, for if Mr. Gladstone
errs in believing them all as sincere and
ardent as he is, Lord Beaconsfield is deceived in believing them all as free from
prejudices as himself. His scepticism dis-
poses him too much to consult their weaknesses rather than their virtues. And it is
the same with things; instead of going to
the bottom of them, he is contented with the
surface, with appearances. In fact, what is
the use of solving problems and satisfying
questions if an end can be reached by some
blowing of trumpets and theatrical ma-
nœuvres? The sceptic willingly does as little as he can, and he does that little in the
easiest possible way. There is something of
the charlatan in him. Witness Lord Beaconsfield in the history of the Congress of
Berlin, and in all the foreign policy of the
last Cabinet. He thinks he has done enough
if he speaks to the imagination. I may add
that he is the same in his books. He is

brilliant, amusing, but superficial. He excites public curiosity for a fortnight. But he does not awaken a profound sentiment or a new idea. His latest novel, 'Endymion,' leaves the impression of a talent which might be promising in a young man, but which in a literary veteran marks, on the contrary, the sorrowful end of a mistaken career."

Besides his numerous volumes of critical work, Scherer is the author of a valuable history on the Franco-Prussian war. But his chief claim to the gratitude of posterity is the fact that he used his taste, his learning, and his tireless industry in the faithful service of classical literature. Wherever in the Babel of voices, his quick ear caught a purer, finer note, he did what he could to rescue it from being drowned in the confusion. He forced a hearing for it, and spread the wholesome influence of its melody. He introduced his countrymen to the works of their great English contemporaries, and so helped in the further dissemination of fruitful thought. He liberated himself from dogma without hatred or violence, because he did it by slow, steady, unaided growth. After the agitation of doubt and inquiry, he reached

the calm of resignation by accepting things
as they are, and recognizing that there are
problems beyond human solution which it is
useless and therefore senseless to state. In
this calm in which he could work at problems which do admit of solution, he tasted
the serenest joy, and as old age came on,
with no abatement of mental vigor and no
chilling of interest in his work, he could
write what few among the old can say:
"What a delicious thing is old age, — old
age approaching or even already come, —
with health, of course, that first condition,
that substratum of all joy, and with faculties
intact enough to spare you the proofs of decay. The passions are stilled, but the feelings may yet be warm. Talent, if there is
any, has gained in acquirements and skill
what it has lost in enthusiasm; time, which
has dissipated the intoxications of youth, has
given in compensation the singular pleasure
of being undeceived. We have learned at
our own expense, to be sure, but we have
learned; and by experience we lay hold
again of the life that is escaping us. We
possess ourselves, and in this self-possession we control the destiny that still remains to be fulfilled."

The whole passage so richly colored by the deep experiences of a truly intellectual life is well worth quoting in full as a *résumé* of Scherer's maturest convictions; but we have space, in conclusion, for its salient features only.

"How many things," he continues, "are only learned with age! . . . Recall to mind the circle of your acquaintances, and ask yourself how many men you know who are in the habit of suspending their judgment, and have the courage, if need be, to confess their ignorance. Impatience with uncertainty leads to generalizations. As we wish to know without learning, or at least to have the illusion that we know, we are not fastidious about the manner in which we arrive at knowledge. The book is judged by one page. Countries are described at first sight. You have met one Englishman, and you tell us what they are all like. If you speak of a current event, you deduce an historical law from it. In short, we deduce and induce with equal arbitrariness, without making the least allowance for the surprises of reality and the sovereignty of fact. Rash generalization is cousin-german of another error, — the idea that men are all alike,

either wholly good or wholly bad, wholly
superior or without merit of any kind, capable of all or capable of nothing. No medium between infatuation and disparagement,
because in order to judge we must have time
to reflect, and we must take the trouble to
analyze. We make shorter work with the
absolute; the mediocre mind takes delight
in the absolute; it is the natural form of
uncultivated thought.

"It must be acknowledged, however, that
distinctions are often difficult to make, even
for a well-trained judgment. We admit easily enough that a great man may not excel
in everything, that he may have, as we say,
the defects of his qualities; but we are loath
to recognize eminent qualities accompanied
by enormous gaps or startling defects, to
admit the union in the same person of a fine
intelligence and a despicable character, or
the union of vigor and affectation in the
same genius. . . . Was ever mind livelier
and fuller of charm than that of Voltaire?
Was ever enthusiasm more entertaining,
good sense more incorruptible? But can the
delight he has given us, and the services he
has rendered, prevent us from admitting that
Voltaire was, on the whole, a pitiable char-

acter, destitute of all sentiment of personal dignity, the most impudent of liars, the most insipid of courtiers, and as much a stranger to patriotism as to decency? . . .

"We confound comfort with happiness, while it is but one of the conditions of happiness. Happiness, though it certainly supposes the satisfaction of our wants, is not the consequence of it. Before all else, happiness is a state of the mind, — a matter of disposition, a philosophy of life, and so much so that we can be happy with few enjoyments, and miserable with the ability to satisfy all our desires. Social progress, then, restored to its true sense, cannot assure the happiness of anybody, and still less can it promise that of the human race. With regard to happiness, it is possible that progress may even defeat its ends; since contentment is a result of wisdom, and wisdom is the fruit of an intellectual culture more refined than that which, according to all appearances, is permitted by democratic levelling. We must be resigned to the fact that for the most part men lose in one direction what they gain in another.

.   .   .   .

"The aim of art is to please, that is to say, to interest, and all means are good by which

success is attained. Nothing is vainer than
the tyranny of rules. I add that art is not
only impatient of rules, but that it under-
goes revolutions. There is one law in particular to which attention has never been
sufficiently paid, and which determines some
periodical crises of taste. Let us consider
for a moment the effects of familiarity. A
poet writes a masterpiece. By this masterpiece he creates a *genre*, founds a school.
Everybody begins to imitate him, until the
vein is exhausted, and the public sated.
This satiety creates the need of something
else, and when this need makes itself felt
we may be sure that it will be satisfied.
Hence, new attempts, new writers, work on
new themes, and so on perpetually, because
interest lies in the unexpected; it is surprise; and surprise, when genius is no longer
able to arouse it in the treatment of familiar
subjects, can come only from innovation. It
must not be concluded, however, that all that
piques curiosity is justifiable by that alone,
or that the old masterpieces necessarily lose
their interest. There are works that aston-
ish and make some noise without deeply
enough interesting the mind to live, and
there are others, on the contrary, that are

rich and deep enough to appear always new.
A writer may come into vogue by writing
vulgarly for the vulgar of his time; but he
can leave his mark in art only by writing
for the men of taste and thought of all ages.

.   .   .   .

"How can any one fail to be struck by the
prominence given to description in contemporaneous literature? It is no longer an
accessory; it has become the very foundation of poetry and romance. Those whom
we rightly esteem the modern masters in
these *genres* — a Balzac, a Hugo — are essentially descriptive. When a page of a
book is praised, or we are told of a new
writer that he has talent, we may be sure
that the eulogy has reference to this sort of
virtuosity. The reason of it is evident. A
writer may have nothing in his brain, and
yet be gifted with an eye that sees forms,
and a hand that can reproduce them. In
confounding literature with the other arts,
we lose sight of the fact that the substance
of the art of composition is language, and
the substance of language is the idea. A
sentence cannot free itself from the necessity
of having a meaning, and the beauty of an
image, or the sonorousness of a word, has no

value but on the condition of remaining in
the service of sense. He only has the right
to hold a pen who has something in his head
or in his heart; and if he feel truly the need
to speak, let him do it with justness, and
in such manner that he can be understood.
The more charm he puts into his manner, so
much the better, assuredly; but the writer is
not absolutely obliged to charm, still less to
entertain; and I can see only the effect of
frivolity avid of amusement in the demands
that are made to-day, without distinction, of
every man who writes a book or an article.
. . . In painting, the means of expression
have a value in themselves; there are admirable pictures whose subject is without interest, as there are some whose coloring
enchants, although the drawing be defective
or the grouping vicious. But intellectual
pleasure is of another order than the pleasure of the eye and ear, and it is to the intellect that we address ourselves when we
write."

III.

ERNEST BERSOT.

" BERSOT, a Moralist," — that is the
title by which Ernest Bersot wished
to be remembered by posterity, and it is the
title of a volume compiled by his friend and
biographer, Edmond Scherer, in which is to
be found a biographical notice of Bersot, and
selections from his volume of Essays entitled "Essays on Literature and Morality."
These essays, and a volume entitled "Educational Questions," are Bersot's most valuable contributions to literature. But it
sometimes happens that a man's life is as
eloquent as anything he has written, that it
teaches us, in the more touching and powerful language of example, the beauty of heroism and the nobleness of a life governed by
the idea of duty. Such a life was Ernest
Bersot's. This man, who said that "the rarest and most charming thing in the world is
perfect simplicity," and whose character bore
testimony to that rarity and charm, — this

man, full of ardor and full of seriousness,
loving the young, loved by them, and devot-
ing his life to their instruction, suffered as
few men are called to suffer in this life, and
yet to the end of it preserved, in the serenity of self-abnegation, his benign and radiant helpfulness to others.

Ernest Bersot was born on the 22d of
August, 1816, and died on the 1st of February, 1880. His birthplace was Surgères,
but he was of Swiss Protestant origin, and
though he had never been in Switzerland,
he had learned to love it from hearing his
father speak of it, and was accustomed to say
that he probably owed to his Swiss origin
his two great passions, — the love of nature
and the love of independence. His father
was a watchmaker, and in 1824 removed with
his family to Bordeaux, where young Ernest
grew up, took a college course, and taught
for a short time. But his apprenticeship for
teaching was finished in the Higher Normal
School of Paris.

We have frank, pleasant glimpses of this
Parisian student-life in his letters written
home. He tells his mother that in Paris he
has the reputation of being "gentle as a
lamb," from which we might infer that this

lamb-like character was something new in him. He adds that in his boarding-house he meets all sorts of people, prejudiced in all sorts of ways, and that he rolls himself into a ball to conceal his asperities.

Once he was invited to dine with one of the professors, a very wealthy man. "I was afraid to go," he writes; "but once there, I watched how the others behaved, so as to do nothing stupid. I talked, told an anecdote now and then, but I was particularly bent on observing. It was very amusing. When dinner was over, some colored bowls with colored glasses were brought in. 'Ah there!' I said to myself, 'is it a float-light?' By no means; it was for washing the mouth and fingers. I waited, I looked, and I executed the operation with cool assurance. There was something that smelt very sweet in the glass of warm water, and one of my inexperienced neighbors drank a good part of it."

After three years in the Normal School, Bersot received his degree of Doctor of Philosophy, and the next year, 1840, he became the secretary of Cousin who was minister of public instruction. At the end of his eight months' service under the Thiers régime, Bersot was appointed professor of philoso-

phy in the College of Bordeaux; but the
freedom of his opinions brought him into
collision with the directors of the College,
and he was forced to resign. His resignation, however, was covered by an appearance of promotion; and the young professor
who dared to think for himself instead of
prudently adopting his opinions, was sent to
Dijon.

Long afterwards, in recollection no doubt
of his own youthful experience, he writes:
"We ask but one thing, and but what is
right, — respect for contrary opinions. We
do not believe what we like, but what we
can; and nobody is responsible but for the
pains he has taken to search for the truth.
When once the mind begins to reflect, it
has no longer the power to stop; it goes on,
impelled by an irresistible force without
knowing what it will find. We cannot express the esteem we have for a man who,
having searched sincerely, and chancing to
fall upon different ideas from those generally received, dares avow it, and renounces
the pleasure so desirable everywhere, but
especially in France, of feeling himself in
harmony with what surrounds him, and exposes himself to the displeasure of those

whom he respects and loves. As the reward of his sincerity, we wish for him the belief in a consoling idea, the happiness of carrying within him an enchanted world in which he can escape the miseries of the outer one; but if he has the misfortune not to possess so happy a belief, if in face of his admitted ideas he has but denials and doubts, he is certainly worthy of respect, for he must love Truth singularly well to follow her even into the deserts."

Bersot remained at Dijon a year, and was then removed to the College at Versailles, where for six years he filled the chair of philosophy. He was very exact in all the details of his duties. Prompt himself in attendance, he required a like promptness of his pupils. He opened his recitations by asking questions on the preceding lesson, then required a summary of the lesson of the day, employing the Socratic method when he found an active mind. While conducting a class he never sat down, but continued walking up and down with his hands behind him. It was the custom, then, to wear a gown at recitation, and the gown annoyed him. One day, in a moment of impatience, he took it off and threw it on a chair. The class smiled. "Excuse me, gentlemen," he explained, "I do it out of respect, I was treading on it."

In explanation, he was brief, clear, easy to follow. He had no mannerisms, and used the natural and varied tones of conversation. Reserved in manner, he made no advances unless attracted by an open mind and good feelings; but he was not unsociable: on the contrary, he greatly enjoyed conversation, music, whist, and gratified these tastes in some houses in Versailles where he was much beloved. Neither did he hold himself aloof from the political interests of his country. There are scholars and men of letters in whom a cosmopolitan spirit, a broad sense of racial unity, destroys or weakens the patriotic sentiment. Bersot did not belong to this class. He was Frenchman to the core. In the Revolution of the 15th of February, 1848, he was one of the volunteers who went to Paris to aid the Assembly. The *coup d'état* grieved him sorely, and he refused to take the oath required of every functionary to support faithfully the Constitution and the President.

"I have an inexpressible horror and disgust," he says, "of all that is going on now, and if I should give my oath in support of such a régime, I should die. . . . I shall leave the University honorably, to return honorably later, it is to be hoped."

He left the University, moved into some inexpensive rooms in the fourth story of a house in the Place d'Armes in Versailles, and reduced his expenses to meet his income from private tutorship and the writing of books. His tastes were simple, and his pleasures therefore within easy reach. An evening with his friends or a ramble in the open air sufficed to make him happy. In the following paragraph he gives us a charming revelation of his love of nature : —

"One starts out full of joy at thought of escaping the daily bustle. At first the mind cannot bestir itself, crowded as it is with a thousand incoherent ideas pressed upon it by the details of life. But it throws off one oppression after another along the road, until finally it succeeds in freeing itself entirely. The exercise of walking sets it in movement, and it goes on in advance of him, lending itself to the chance impressions which objects bring to it; the floating cloud, the bird flying from a branch, the ant hastening to work, the lizard concealing itself in the brambles, the flower whose perfume betrays it, the murmur of water, the roaring of waves and wind, the torment of the trees in its power, the grand silence of the fields, the mysterious hum that proceeds from nature, — all these impressions, that succeed one another and penetrate him with the great life of nature, efface the troubled image of the world he has quitted. The soul grows simpler, and imagines a world in which it could always live as now, happy and free. Yes, the soul has wings in these gracious moments. These walks in the open air, under the open sky, make life more buoyant, and the thoughts that are born in them have a strength and charm to be found nowhere else."

In 1853 Bersot published his "Essay on Providence," and his volume on "Mesmer and Animal Magnetism." Two years later his "Studies on the Eighteenth Century" appeared, and in 1857 his "Letters on Education" were successively published in pamphlet form. During this same year, after a short journey in Italy, he became acquainted with Saint-Marc Girardin, by whom he was subsequently introduced to journalism.

His contributions to the "Journal des Débats" enabled him to give up his private tutorship. The work was congenial, and introduced him to congenial men. He enjoyed the praise that came to him on the quality of his work, but he was not intoxicated by it. "I have this peculiarity," he writes home: "it seems to me as if the compliments paid me were not addressed to me, and I am never elated by thoughts of my merits. I think only of what is wanting in me; of the uncertainty and transitory character of the inspiration that dictated a happier passage than another; of the necessity of working and increasing my reputation; of human instability. Only I am very glad to be doing a man's work, and I can never exhaust this pleasure."

"To do a man's work," not only in literary and educational service, but in kindly offices to one's fellow-men, is not always characteristic of scholars, but it was characteristic of Bersot. During the Franco-Prussian War he visited the wounded French in the hospitals, going from bed to bed, offering his services to the unfortunate soldiers, writing their letters, or bringing them news of their absent friends. He was assisted in this benevolent work by his young friend, Arnold Scherer, son of Edmond Scherer.

There was nothing lukewarm in Bersot's patriotism. No one could laugh at the foibles of Frenchmen more heartily, or write of them with a kindlier irony than he; but for France, the nation, the mother-country, he had an inextinguishable and fervent love, and when the Prussians attacked her, he was thoroughly obstinate in his optimism about the result. "I remember," says Scherer, "that he was angry with me and avoided me several days, because I believed the news that Strasburg was taken, and to him it was a sort of religion to doubt this catastrophe."

In 1871 Bersot was made director of the Normal High School at Paris, and continued to fulfil the duties of this office until his death. He was then, and had long been, suffering from the terrible disease that was to carry him away, and which made life a punishment. In 1864 the first symptoms of a cancer appeared on his cheek, and the daily progress of this frightful malady rendered him an object of fear and pity to all; yet he accepted his agony as an inevitable fact, and employed all his strength and all his courage to bear it like a man. Never once did he complain to his friends; never once did he betray to them the slightest anxiety. Scherer tells us that he "dissimulated so carefully what he felt, he so evidently turned every subject of conversation touching himself, that his friends were obliged to enter into this conspiracy of silence. . . . It was not stoicism. We find in his language neither exaggeration, effort, nor pride. Neither was it pious resignation with its optimistic tendency. It was something simpler and more natural; man enduring misery, agony, trembling in the presence of destruction, yet lifting himself above his sufferings by the faculty he preserves of contemplating them. He did not deny them, which would have been rodomontade; he did not transform them into pledges of future felicity, which is the rôle of piety; but he felt the singular and bitter satisfaction of rendering clearly to himself an account of his destiny. Such are the 'consolations of philosophy.' I have often observed that this kind of defence against pain and death is the privilege of very cultivated minds. Literature can do much in this. It seems that association with the finest minds communicates to us an elevation from the heights of which we can judge life more serenely."

Bersot had not only strength for himself, but strength and encouragement for the young under his care. "This mutilated face," says one of his pupils, "had a smile for us to the end. . . . 'Why abuse life? Life is good;' I still hear the sound and the accent of these words that he liked to repeat, and then he recounted the delights of life, and the simpler pleasures; a beautiful walk, an entertaining book; — then the real blessings; the love of those who surround us, the sacredness of those whom we have lost; and, lastly, the great duties; devotion to a noble cause, the accomplishment of some useful and obscure task. We left him, ashamed of ourselves, but more tranquil and stronger."

Doubtless few can read the report of Bersot's physician without feeling, as this pupil did, ashamed in the consciousness of cowardice in the endurance of afflictions far less severe; and more tranquil and stronger, in the knowledge that human fortitude, human obedience to duty, can rise to so sublime a height. For that reason we give some extracts from the report, painful as it is: —

"From the first months of 1879 the cancer by which M. Bersot had been attacked for fourteen years perforated the cheek, and had eaten into the gums and nerves of the maxillary bones. From this moment our poor friend had not an hour's rest. He suffered without truce. The pain was continuous, and increased every day by several crises which he attributed to decayed teeth. We dared not undeceive him, and he did not think of having them extracted, because for seven years, that is, since the first operation, his two jaws were absolutely immovable, and a second operation would have been followed by consequences involving a long time for recovery, and he did not wish to be taken from the care of his school."

Once, when a new treatment had been pro· posed, and it was necessary for him to cease his school supervision, he would not consent to it until after the classification of the new candidates was over; and then, when that day came, he demanded a respite of his doctor because he had to console the disappointed candidates. "I cannot shut my door on them," he cried; "counsel and encouragement often decide a career. These poor children deserve it. They have worked so hard."

When the end drew near, he said to his doctor: "I am not afraid of death, and I am preparing for it.   At the rate this disease is making, I have probably three more months to live.   I shall see the beginning of the new promotions.   I shall write an article on Cousin that will be abused, and then my work is done."

"Oh, no!" replied the doctor, "fortunately the end is not so near."

"So much the worse," was the reply. "My life is painful to me now.   In the past three years, since the operation, I have had a great deal of pleasure in taking part in social life again, and in seeing my friends. But the disease has come back.   At first I concealed it by putting it under my hand or on the shaded side.   But now I dread the houses where there are children.   I am afraid of their questions about the wound in my cheek.   Of late, I have refused all invitations.   I have gone only to the minister of instruction and to the institute.   I ought to have given up going there.   In the evening I quitted the school secretly; I went round the Pantheon, or even down by the Seine.   Well, for five months now, I have not gone out in broad day, — I who at Versailles passed the day in the woods."

"This is the only complaint," adds the doctor, "that I ever heard from him."

"Since the second of December," continued Bersot to his physician, "I pray every night, and the habit of it is such that my prayer, always the same, comes to my lips, though sometimes my thoughts are elsewhere. 'My God,'" here he paused, "yes, I address God, and yet this term is very obscure to me; I believe firmly in liberty, in duty, in immortality. The effort of thought, the struggle to discipline the soul, all the work of a life cannot be lost; but the idea of God seems to me less and less distinct, but I address him: 'My God, save France and liberty, and let me see those I love again.'"

"Those who saw M. Bersot during this time could not believe that they were face to face with a man struck by death and conscious of it. He received you in his handsome school-office seated before the chimney and near his desk. He had arranged the light so that it illuminated only the sound half of his face. A cordial smile welcomed you. Then rapidly, as if to avoid all questions about himself, he entered into the heart of the conversation. How many efforts he employed to conceal the pain he felt! I have seen him continue talking in the midst of a neuralgic paroxysm. That is not all; his voice, which no longer issued from his mouth but from the gaping wound in his cheek, grew less and less distinct and sometimes hollow, and so, in order not to weary his listeners, he tried to articulate distinctly, and exhausted himself more and more."

He worked up to the last week of his life, fulfilling his duties, continuing to interest himself in all that was going on. "I have never felt my thought clearer," he said. "They say my last writings are my best, thanks to my solitude, no doubt. The prettiest flowers grow only in the wildest woods."

A brave, beautiful soul; a man who did the work of a man and felt his joy in it; a man stricken in his prime, and bearing mutely the agony of the stroke, lest a cry of pain should mar the beauty and value of the gift to others of what was best and strongest in himself, — that was Ernest Bersot. In his essays on "Happiness" and on "Pleasure and Pain," he touches, with a fine irony and rare good sense, the various mental attitudes towards the calamities of human life, and lets us into the secret of his wise courage, — his philosophy of life.

"There is a silly optimism," he writes, "which imagines that everything that happens is for the best; and not satisfied with this sanctimonious contentment, it must find in every particular circumstance some special argument to prove that what has happened is better so than otherwise. There is also a class of pious persons who are provided with so much resignation that in the very heat of their friendship for you they are quite prepared to give you up, and you might die without fear of causing them the slightest pain. I admire these optimists and devotees very much, and I envy them their peace of mind; but if I were choosing my friends, I should very likely choose them of another sort; for by an egotism from which it is difficult to purify the human heart, we suffer a little at the thought that our friends would not take our death very much to heart, but on the contrary find it a natural and proper event. It is well enough to be consoled, but they are too much consoled.

"Fortunately, the world knows another virtue, the resignation of truly religious

souls, convinced that God exists, that he is
perfectly wise and good even when he sends
some great sorrow, bowing under his decrees, and adoring, while they weep, the
hand that smites them. Some, in a trans-
port of heroism, go beyond this resignation.
As I write I have in mind a thought of Joubert's: 'We must love the gifts and the re-
fusals of God, — love what he wills and
what he does not will.' . . .

"Let us now consider ancient stoicism,
which sees no good but virtue, and no evil
but vice. It is a sublime paradox that nature
denies. Not even the heights and depths
of the joys of virtue can take the place of
everything. Virtue may make us happy in
one direction, and leave us miserable in
other ways. The sages justly said: 'The
happiness which virtue procures is the only
one which is always in our own hands, the
only one that does not corrupt; the fullest
happiness that we are permitted to enjoy on
earth.' But reason reasons in vain; virtue
does not relieve those that suffer; it does not
feed the hungry, give water to the thirsty,
nor the power to love to those who hunger
and thirst to love.

"The truth is, that pain is simply an inevitable fact.   Given the laws of organization and life, — our faculties, their limits and their infinite aspirations, — and pleasure and pain inevitably follow.   The truth is, too, that once fronting pain, man ought to act as a man, exert all his energy and all his pride. He suffers because he is an animal; but since he is something more than that, he suffers in a manner peculiar to himself. That is what seems true to me.   I only ask that it shall not be said that pain was made for the use man makes of it; that it was created for his advantage.   To say that, is to abuse final causes. . . .

"Man is not born to be happy, but he is born to be a man at his risks and perils. How good it is to feel one's self under this law!   How much virtue there is in the thought; how much tranquillity and strength!   We must go to life, therefore, as we go to a fire, — bravely, without asking how we shall come back; and if we are mortally wounded, — well, for my part, I believe there is some one who sees our wounds."

Criticism was rather the accident than the business of Bersot's life.   He was essentially an educator.   The progress of mental development, the springs of human action, the influence of the experiences of life, interested him profoundly, and in literature he preferred what fed this interest. No man to whom life has bared her real tragedies can find tears for mock pain, or joy in the heartless stripping of the veil of ideality from the nakedness of life. Therefore, in Bersot, solidity of judgment was united with a fine, poetical instinct that made him keenly sensitive to the absence of enduring charm and merit in the so-called realism of his day. He sums up its shallowness and defects in the criticism of a popular author of his time, from which the following extracts are taken: —

"According to M. Champfleury, realism, in short, is the reproduction of quite crude reality, independent of its interest which is a false god. . . . M. Champfleury does not clearly enough distinguish between the real and the dull. In literature, insignificant reality is of no account. In order to merit description, a passing event or a passing face must say something; if they do not, they are nothing. Putting your head out of the window is not all that is necessary in order to see a drama; because a face or a crowd of faces is not worth the trouble of reproducing unless a soul is revealed in it; — a soul under the sway of some passion, whether it be joy, sorrow, hope, fear, pity, fury, or heroism.

". . . I must thank the author for a service he has rendered me. Until now, I had believed that it was a difficult thing to write a novel, and that a realistic novel was especially difficult because it must be supported by observations taken on the scene. But I am reassured. I need not run all over the world to study human nature. I can study it by my fireside in the Police Gazette. After such study I shall be very stupid if, in taking the flower of the crimes, I cannot write my little novel. I must thank M. Champfleury and his disciples for yet another obligation, which they do not suspect having rendered. Ordinary life in itself is dull enough, but after reading certain realistic novels everything seems poetic, by comparison, — the very furnishings of one's room, the utensils of housekeeping, the passers-by on the street.

. . . .

"Where art thou, O poetry, that we may refresh ourselves in thy living waters? Art thou but an illusion that God has given to console us in life, or rather, art thou not life itself, since thou art the inspiration towards something better? The day is dark; the clouds gather; the rain falls; at last it ceases. Earth and air drink the water and nothing remains of it but one drop on a leaf. The sun comes out, shines on it, and it bursts into a blaze of color. That drop of water, that fiery ray is poetry, the charm of the world. . . .

"There is another realism than that of which we have been speaking. Human intelligence has always been divided into two classes. The one class of mind, curious, observing, rejoicing in seeing what exists, cannot be sated with the infinite variety of nature; wholly absorbed in this research, it is less critical. Every form that exists pleases it, as one more form in the universe. The other class of mind, belonging to men of imagination and sentiment, dreams of a more perfect nature, and criticises what it sees. It has preferences, antipathies; it would suppress certain forms if it could, and it excludes them from art.

"Men of the first class love what is, — that is, reality. They are the realists. Those of the second class love what ought to be,

—the ideal. They are idealists. What I am saying is old as the world. I am ashamed to say it, and only say it to those who have forgotten it. In philosophy, it is the opposition of Aristotle and Plato; in painting, these classes are represented by the Dutch and the Italians; in politics, by Montesquieu and Rousseau; in literature, by Shakespeare and Racine. I confess my weakness for the latter class. But, great God! what a loss we should sustain in losing the former — what treasures of science! what marvels of observation!

. . . .

"Man does many things that animals do; but whatever he does, he does humanly; he brings to its performance some one of these things: moderation, intelligence, feeling, delicacy, conscience, devotion. The realists suppress these things. There are two realities in man; they leave the one and take the other which they call reality. By what right? As if good were not as real as evil! As if the remorse of Phèdre were not as real as her passion! What! the timidity of a heart that fears to confess that it loves, the combat, the scruple about violating an engaged faith, the grief at having been found

wanting in it, the shame of yielding one's
self to unworthy creatures, the desire to rise
again out of this shame, — is n't all that
real? Is there anything more real, more
human? Is n't it we ourselves? And what
a happy inspiration in novelists, who are
supposed to search movement and life, to retrench all that! There is a story of virtue, of its efforts to maintain itself, a story
as varied as characters and circumstances;
there is a story of passion, of its birth, progress, transports, a story told again and again
since the world began, always new and destined to be always new, for the same sun
does not illuminate the same world twice;
but there is also a love which has no story,
and this is the love you have chosen to write
about.

.   .   .   .

"In searching the cause of these moral, artistic, and philosophical eccentricities an idea
occurs to me. It seems to me unjust to attribute the same value to all the thoughts
and feelings of a nation. Some of them are
essential, their foundation being human nature. Others are transitory; they do not
proceed from the true nature of man, but
from something accidental. A physical mal-

ady, for example, gives to our ideas and feelings a character that passes away with the
disease.   In a paroxysm of fever, or a crisis
in certain organic affections, we are no
longer ourselves.   The soul, too, has its
crises, in which one writes 'René' or
'Lélie.'   Then the crisis passes, nature's
equilibrium is restored; life resumes its normal course; the patient comes to himself, and
is astonished at what he has been.   Why
should not nations suffer from these disorders?   Why do we not distinguish in them
what is their mind, their real soul, from
what is simply a fit, a crisis, a transitory
state of mind?   Nations as well as individuals have their periods of sickness and
health.   In health the aim is fixed; the
road lies straight in the sunlight; the sight
is clear; the step firm; the whole body in
harmony, is disposed for action, feels itself
move and live.   In sickness, the aim is concealed or shifting, the road uncertain, the
step faltering; a false light troubles the
eyes and changes the color and form of
things; the sentiment of reality is lost, and
the patient moves as if in a dream.   If we
are in this condition, at present, it is but a
trial, and the solid genius of this nation is

capable of enduring many such trials. I am
no longer alarmed at the perturbation of its
feelings and thoughts. It is a languor, a
crisis from which it will recover."

All Bersot's criticism is marked by the
qualities of this extract, — gentle irony, and
clear, rapid, firm, and serious statement of
fact interspersed with jets of enthusiasm.
He is warm, but not passionate; serious,
but neither dull nor sad. There are no dark
corners in his mind. A steady light burns
there; he can give account of what he feels
and knows, and he values this light.

"The Greeks," he writes, "were enamoured
of physical light, and in dying bade it touching adieus. We, who have not their limpid
ether, are enamoured of intellectual light.
Our intelligence recognizes it, moves freely,
and rejoices in it. It struggles and suffers
in darkness; it is restless until day dawns.
That is the eternal foundation of the French
intellect. . . . In France we do not willingly lose sight of earth. If any one ventures into space, we look at him, but we do
not follow him. We think more of seeing
clearly that our wealth is on a firm basis
than of increasing it. We even consent to
diminish its bulk for the sake of getting rid

of the false coin. . . . Clearness is intelligence. . . . We are always glad, when, after
a mist which obscures and confuses everything, objects begin to be distinguished and
to take their true form and their true being.
We are glad, too, when an idea which was
vague in us begins to clear up, when day
begins in our thought, and the true nature
and the true reason of things appear to us in
their natural order."

Bersot loved simplicity as he loved clearness, and no trickery of rhetoric, no tinsel
or tirade deceived him into seeing merit
where there was none. He praised "simple
beauty, the discreet beauty that does not
make a display of its charms, and is unknown except to some true souls like itself."
He says somewhere: "When all men around
you are running after riches, you must be
firm to resist their example; when all are
running after what glitters, it takes courage
to keep alive at the bottom of your heart the
unknown and solitary flame. But it warms
you, and at this ruddy fireside of those who
have scarcely any other here on earth, rest
is to be found, and poetry is sometimes a
visitor."

He sees clearly that the less delicate the

instrument whose sounds we wish to evoke, the harder we must strike. "When we speak to the public," he writes, "we need an affirmative tone, for it cannot conceive doubt; we need a great appearance of logic, for it sees but one principle at a time; a great deal of sentiment, for it has an honest instinct; a great deal of imagery, for it is taken by the senses. With the public, it is less a question of striking justly than of striking hard. In objects which are to be exposed to the people, the necessary features are strong proportions, salient outlines, and a simple and pronounced character in which are no delicacies to be lost. The metaphysical, the gigantic, and the prophetic style were invented for the people, and have succeeded."

Better than any other, he knows all the weakness and peculiarities of his own public, and gives us the following good-humored inventory of them with its accompaniment of timely and sensible advice.

"One of the first characteristics of the French is restlessness. We are impatient. We can suffer no delay between the conception of an idea and its complete application. . . . We put on seven-league boots to take four steps. . . . Another of our weaknesses

is a love of novelty. When two Frenchmen meet, the first question infallibly is:
'What's the news?' With a melancholy
air, the other replies: 'Nothing. Nothing
new has happened.' But on the other hand,
if there is something to tell, what contentment, what ardor in asking and affirming!
How we run from house to house! How
quickly we make the circuit to comment, discuss, and learn the general impression, and
what we ought to think of it! Every morning, on awakening, we feel the need of an
occupation of this kind for the whole day.
It is on these conditions alone, that we think
we truly live. And we are not exclusive.
Give us anything you like, — a new play, a
new novel, a new author, a duel, a political
question, a theological quarrel, a riot, a
sermon, an assassination, — anything. We
should be unable to resist for any length of
time the exhausting effects of so much excitement, if we were in reality profoundly
moved by every occurrence, but, fortunately,
we take good care of ourselves. In every
event, we always keep in reserve a little sensibility for to-morrow's use. Very likely
we are less interested in affairs than in what
is said of them. Be they what they may,

sad or disastrous, we feel great relief in the
discussion of them.　Men and affairs are the
ceaseless topic of French conversation.　Our
novels and dramatic literature thrive on accidents, and the press that lives on the public stimulates its passions to make itself
necessary to its readers.　It collects and
illustrates sensational facts to gratify sharpened curiosity.　It would prefer to fabricate
sensations rather than to do without them;
and if it happens that a murder is wanting,
it has lost a day.

"The nation fabricates its politics as it
does its novels and dramas.　It wants to
move.　It wants something new and something dramatic, some lightning strokes, some
unforeseen blows, perpetual shifting of scen-
ery.　With this taste, we have a theatrical
and romantic politics.　We wake to a surprise every morning, — to a grand combat
between the opposition and the government;
a combat on the street, in the press, or in
the Chamber.　At bottom, our nation fears
nothing as it fears *ennui*.　Rather than be
bored, she is capable of rushing into all
sorts of adventures at the risk of cruel suffering, — of rushing into a revolution just to
see how she will come out of it.　How com-

pletely she has forgiven Napoleon I., because he made her live by her imagination. He bled her, and she adored him. Go thou and preach wisdom to her. Talk to her of a well-ordered life, of domestic happiness. Tell her that in doing a little every day, we shall find at the end of a year or of years that we have done much. . . .

"If France wishes only to amuse herself and the world, let her indulge herself in these whims; but if she aims at being happy and respected, she must give them up. Let her apply all her intelligence and passion to solving the great modern problem of constituting a free and civilized democracy. . . .

"What we French have served our apprenticeship at, or rather, wherein we excel, is in demolishing governments. At the Versailles Museum is to be seen Horace Vernet's fine painting of the assault on Constantinople. How those soldiers climb! What ardor and fury they show! At the rate at which they are going they might scale the heavens. They are our countrymen, — these fellows. We French are born for attack. In an assault on the government what pleasure we take in the epigrams, the fine speeches, the vigorous and malicious articles,

the cleverness shown in tripping up an oppo-
nent, the lessening of good and increasing of
evil; and so history, poetry, romance, and the
drama go to war; it is a terrible outbreak.
Nothing can resist it. This is our incontest-
able talent. Doubtless that is why we so generally claim to be well versed in politics. But
it is a remarkable fact that we have no states-
men. There are not many of us who would
dare climb on a locomotive and start it going,
for it is not solely a question of going; it is
also a question of being able to stop without
an explosion. On the contrary, in political
matters everybody is ready to climb on the
engine. It is true that in the first case a
man only risks blowing up himself; while,
in the second case, he risks blowing up other
people, which is a very different thing. . . .

". . . Democracy has a lesson to learn;
the lesson taught by indefatigable personal
activity, by conscientious resistance, uncon-
querable resolution; by that, in short, which
makes the character of a man; and it is character, it is men that we need, if we do not
wish the elements of our nation to be but a
multitude of atoms brought together by the
winds from the four corners of heaven and
scattered again at their pleasure.

"For my part, I know of no more pressing problem, warned in some sort by the place where I am writing, — one of those sand dunes which the sea deposits on its shores. Blown by the wind, they advance from year to year swallowing up whatever they find before them. A man has stopped the advance of this one. He has planted trees whose deep roots fix the sand and resist the wind. Life has been stronger than the elements. Let us try his plan on this shifting soil of democracy, tormented in every way by its own violence and that of its masters. Let us sow men here; not ancient sages who fold their arms and resign themselves to being buried alive; but living, breathing, acting men who want to take their place in the sun, hold it fast, and extend it.

"Make democracy stable by stirring up in every man that composes it, a personal conscience, the sentiment of right and the courage to defend it."

Wherever the strong and helpful word is needed, Bersot is ready to say it; but the work in which all the alertness and sagacity of his mind found full play for its action is in the education of the young. He brought to this work not only sagacity and alertness,

but tact, firmness, kindness. The professor
never drowned the man in him. He had a
horror of routine. He did not wish the
pupil to be a machine, nor the professor "a
machine to make machines." He had the
genius of a great commander who is not
bound by the rules of his tactics, but can
fearlessly break them in an emergency, because he is greater than they, and can see
over and beyond them into the result he is
aiming at. He never forgot that he was not
working on paper, or inert, yielding material, but on living, resistant human souls;
and that in such work an ounce of practice
is worth a pound of theory. He strongly
opposed that requirement in the educational
system of France which forced a child at
thirteen to choose between a scientific or a
literary course of study. He recognizes the
excellence of the theory of education in special directions, but observes that it errs in
practice, children of thirteen not being safe
judges of their aptitudes or even of their inclinations. Besides, he does not believe in
a divorce in education; both literary and
scientific instruction are necessary to a complete education.

"An educated man," he writes, "ought to

know something of letters and something of science, in order to be interested in all intellectual subjects. He ought not to be a stranger to the charms of literature, and with regard to the marvels of industry, steam, light, electricity, he ought to be able to follow an explanation at least to the point where it is lost in formulas.

.　.　.　.　.　.　.　.

"The gymnasium knows the importance of general exercise. A single exercise is not enough. Effort and varied effort is demanded. Strength and suppleness are not given to any one member of the body in view of any one particular service, but, what is better, vigor and skill are given to every part of it. The same end should be attained in education; therefore we should not separate literary and scientific instruction, if we aim at the perfection of the human mind."

Here follows a quotation of the scene from Molière's "Malade imaginaire," in which the doctor counsels his patient to cut off one arm, because it takes to itself all the nourishment, and prevents the other from profiting by it; and to take out the right eye because the left one will see the better for

not being distracted by the interference of
the other.

"I am for the right eye and the left eye,"
adds Bersot, pithily. "With our two eyes we
have not any too much light to see well by,
in this world."

He thinks that if education does anything,
it ought especially to give the desire to
learn; it ought to excite an appetite, create
tastes. He counsels the study of the classics, if we wish to nourish what is healthiest
and give to the young that taste for simplicity without which there is no true grace
either in life or in literature.

Reading was for a long time regarded in
University life as lost time or a danger.
The student was expected to get his mental
nutriment either at the hands of his professors or from his text-books. Such an idea
aroused Bersot's indignation. "Lost time?"
he cries; "does reading not nourish and
awaken the mind? Does it not make it feel
that it lives? A danger? Everything is dangerous for an inert soul, but when it is living, the torrent of life sweeps away every
danger." He especially counsels moderate
tasks and wide and varied reading as the
chief means of intellectual culture.

"The understanding of all things, criticism which gives to each thing its value, richness and elevation of taste and sentiment, — that is civilization."

In teaching, Bersot addressed himself to the intelligence and not to the memory of his pupils. He praises the chief educational maxim of Pascal's father, which was always to keep his child above his work. "He whose work taxes all his faculties," he adds, "is an artisan. He who is above his work does that, and is capable of something more. The mind is not a shop, it is an instrument. . . . Children are never so much interested in what others do as in what they do themselves, and the best professor is he who gets the most work out of them. The best conducted class is that which least resembles a lecture-course, but most one of those walks or journeys in which a master full of authority, knowledge, discretion, and kindness for youth, awakens his pupil's curiosity, teaches him to see, to search, to find, tries his judgment and corrects it in all circumstances, not imposing the stiffness of military drill on this mobile spirit, but yielding to its movements in order to form them. The interest given to instruction is the best disci-

pline; and when a teacher has associated his
memory with that of the first work of dawn-
ing intelligence, he need not fear that his
memory will be effaced."

He sees clearly that a fact is not necessarily educating in itself; that it may lie
dead or dormant in the mind, and that it is
not until it sets up a ferment, a growth, a
living activity, that it becomes truly educating. The fact must be converted into an
emotion before it becomes a leaven. This
is what he means by the distinction he
makes between soul and body in the study
of any science. "Facts and truths are the
body. The faculty that embraces all these
truths, reflects on them to understand them
and to find more of them, is the soul. You
may know all the facts of history, all the
truths of philosophy, all the propositions of
geometry, and have neither the soul of philosophy nor the soul of mathematics; for
with all your facts, your philosophy may be
lacking in method, and a true feeling of the
nature of the problems you discuss: you may
lack penetration in history, and in mathematics you may be wanting in the logic that
links the last propositions to the first, the
scruples about continually demanding the

reason of what you do, the patience to go on
step by step, the power to abstract and gen-
eralize, the skill in constructions for rendering demonstrations easier, and address in
solving problems. . . . Without this soul
what is science? What is art? Or rather,
is there a science or an art without it?"

Bersot's enthusiasm was not of the perfer-
vid, transitory kind whose flame is fed by
illusion, and dies out when the illusion is
dissipated. His enthusiasm was a mild,
steady heat founded on good sense and judgment. He had no dream of human perfecti-
bility to be realized by universal education.
He knew that the clay given him to work
with was of various degrees of fineness and
coarseness, and that he could not make
porcelain vases out of all of it. Moreover,
he knew that the finer clay is of extreme
rarity, and that it is not always possible to
distinguish it at first sight. For this reason
he felt that public instruction ought to address itself to all, but more particularly
ought "to occupy itself with ordinary minds
that form the immense majority; ought to
take by the hand pupils of common capacity
and teach them to walk, and lead them as
far as possible. Those who have wings will

fly. The influence of instruction on superior minds is commonly exaggerated. The
fact is that they always find their road, even
if they do not form themselves quite unaided. Their original genius develops even
under masters who oppose them. They go
out like Voltaire from the schools of Jesuits."

One of the true problems of education, he
felt to be the finding of a medium between
the rigid discipline of the regiment and the
softness, the enervating laxity of domestic
indulgence. There was a cleanness, an un-
selfishness in Bersot's love of the young, a
wholesome tonic quality in it, exempt from
any vanity, any wish to flatter weaknesses in
order to create a liking for himself, a wisdom that looked to the best interests of
youth, which made his love what all love
should be, but alas! is not, — a strength, a
safety, and a lasting joy. With this pure,
unselfish ideal of parental love, he found it
difficult to understand the selfish instinct
which goes by the nobler name of love, and
is so often the bane of children. "One of
the astonishing things of this age," he
writes, "is the softness of parents. They
wish to be loved, and what is better? But
they no longer see that in order to be loved

lastingly, they must first be respected; and that no one is respected who surrenders a legitimate part of the authority he has received; that to be loved lastingly, it is necessary, if need be, to consent not to be loved for a moment. This courage is properly the father's part; but by his absorption in business, the management of the family often falls upon the mother; and to me there are few spectacles more touching than that of a mother who, eager to be loved, eager to please her son and to satisfy his slightest caprices, stops, and, seeing clearly the solid interest of that son some place where he does not see it, takes the authority, while her heart bleeds in exercising it. That is heroism. . . . In education it is necessary to know how to work, how to accept discipline, and how to sacrifice pleasure to duty."

Duty, — that is a good word with which to close our study of Ernest Bersot. It was the ruling idea of his life; it was followed without asceticism or display, in sunshine and in shadow; and because the world has need of it, the memory of his faithfulness and courage will not die.

IV.

SAINT-MARC GIRARDIN.

FEW who have been associated for any length of time with persons of a fastidious and highly nervous type, intellectual yet destitute of the grasp and strength of the highest intellect, can have missed noting in them a lack of repose and harmony, and a morbid capacity for suffering from trifles. Instead of meeting their vexations with a toss of the hand, as one brushes a fly from the face, they meet them with violence, as if in a hand-to-hand conflict with giants, and suffer more from the exhaustion of the conflict than from the original evil. There is nothing of the Spartan about them. They make their sensibility their chief title to distinction, and instead of concealing the fox and the wound, they run about showing the marks of his teeth.

To go out from the influence of this nervous irritability that poisons the very springs of human joy, into that of those broad, serene, outward-looking not inward-looking natures, is like leaving a wine-cellar swarming with gnats and flies and lined with cobwebs, for the open air, placid sunshine, and genial exhilaration of an afternoon in early May. Slowly the flushed cheek loses its heat; the pulse slackens its feverish rapidity. We no longer pant, but breathe deep, slow draughts of wholesome air, and in proportion as vigor returns, joy, calm but deep, returns with it.

Now, just such a wholesome influence in literature is Saint-Marc Girardin after the Rousseaus, Chateaubriands, and Senancours. To him was given the task of freeing the youth of his time from romantic superstitions; and he did his work without iconoclastic violence, but with such calm appeals to reason and experience that it has permanent value.

Saint-Marc Girardin, whose real name was simply Marc Girardin, was born in Paris in 1801, and died from a stroke of apoplexy at Morsang-sur-Seine in 1873.

At the age of twenty-seven he became one of the contributors to the "Journal des Débats," and on the accession of Louis Philippe he was appointed to succeed Guizot as professor of history at the Sorbonne. His

predilection for literature induced him to
exchange his professorship of history for
that of literature. His popularity as a lec-
turer crowded his class-room with eager listeners, and the literary quality of his work
was so high that in 1844 he was elected a
member of the French Academy.

For forty-five years he continued his association with the University, and his most
important publications were the result of his
work in the class-room. Hence the domi-
nant note in him, — the appeal of experience
to the errors of judgment and the falsely
grounded enthusiasms of immaturity and
ignorance. Hence, too, the enduring value
of his work, for each generation passes
through the errors of the youth-time of that
which preceded it, and the warning voice of
experience is therefore always timely. We
all begin by loving disorder and lawlessness
as elements of growth and liberty. It is a
long time before we learn to love law, and to
recognize its primal importance, — to know
that, in fact, it is the very foundation of life,
growth, and freedom, — that the sun keeps
his course in the heavens, the earth her
miracle of seed-time and harvest, and the
human body its soundness, by obedience to

law, — that a broken law means pain, disorder, and, if persisted in, ends in ruin. It is a long time before we learn to look outward, not inward, — before we learn not to mistake our own bitter personal experiences for universal calamity, and before we know that cynicism and pessimism have no place in healthy human existence. It is a long time before we cease wishing to attempt the establishment of a new system of morals in which individual desire shall be the only recognized basis, and to cease to find in existing social institutions the cause of individual wretchedness. Sometimes we never do outgrow these errors of immaturity, and if to the power of feeling our wretchedness be added the gift of expressing it, we put our wailing into books or pamphlets, and find a like-minded public that will call it literature.

In this strait it were good for us if a Saint-Marc Girardin could fall in our way. These tumors of self-torturing vanity need puncturing; and in him a good, a kindly physician is at hand. He does not frighten us in the manner of a charlatan, by a violent and exaggerated picture of our condition. He is not so severe that we prefer to die of our malady rather than to be cured in so painful a manner. He is a brother who lays hold of our hand and speaks in firm but good-humored accents. He makes us forget ourselves in the broad outlook on humanity that he opens before us. He sets a faithful mirror in our path, and we catch a perfect image of our pitiful selves, and, disgusted at our weakness and ugliness, we resolve to be something else, if it be yet in our power to change.

What he is in his books, Saint-Marc Girardin was in his life and character. A scholar, well versed in German and Italian, but no pedant. First of all, a man of activity, full of life and light.

Bersot, who knew him intimately for more than twenty years, says of him in his introduction to one of the editions of Girardin's "Jean Jacques Rousseau": "To be seen at his best, Girardin must be seen in intimacy. He had perfect simplicity; in social intercourse the most congenial, the gentlest of men, with whom endless chats were possible, — true chats in that full liberty and full security in which one dares say everything. His conversation was not monologue. . . . He let subjects come and go as they would, persisting in nothing, lending himself to everything. He gave wit to all with whom he talked; he had no wish to shine, but a desire to be agreeable which made him so. . . .

"No one was ever less of a dreamer. At Paris, where he lived as little as possible, work, business, society occupied him. In the country he was in his library at an early hour, preparing his lectures, writing his books or his articles. He took his rest in going about his estate, the park, the kitchen-garden, the stable, seeing that everything was in order, — giving instructions as to what should be done, never tiring of being in the open air where there was something to do, — seeing that stones were cleared away, trees planted, protecting them from injury, observing the defences that succeeded best, attentive to those that were languishing, and renewing those that were dead, familiar with the age and history of each one, — enchanted with his work. He loved active country life. He had a horror of the vague. . . .

"He was a born moralist. One always felt in his lectures and in his conversations the man who knew men. He knew them so well that he demanded perfection of no one; and if, along with some essential qualities he discovered some defects, he was indulgent towards the defects, —taking the whole, putting the good to the account of the individual, and the evil to the account of humanity. If a servant were recommended as faultless to him, he refused to take him, confident that he must have some vice; but, on the contrary, once he knew just what failing he had, he would take him, knowing what to expect and how to defend himself. This knowledge of human nature rendered him exceedingly easy to meet. . . . Then, too, he was exceedingly sensitive to individual worth. He made a distinction between being something and being somebody. To be something is not much; but to be somebody is worth the trouble of being, and that is a privilege not granted to every one. So when he said that a man was somebody, it was great eulogy; he had set him apart from the others whom he classed in mass as the indistinguishables.

"His large, clairvoyant experience made him take events very much as he took men; that is, with a fine indulgence. He believed in what he called the caprices of

events.   He thought that matters nearly
always turn out differently from what we
think they will; that the unforeseen plays a
prominent rôle in the world, and that accident is master of affairs.   So when things
went well, he did not trust himself to them,
and if they went ill, he was not disquieted;
he waited. . . . One day, when we were
chatting on a subject that was giving us
some anxiety, he said to me: 'What saves
this country is that there is a great fecun-
dity of abortions.' . . . He was a family
man, and found in domestic life two forces
that he never separated, and without which
he could not conceive life, — love and duty."

The genius of Saint-Marc Girardin can be
summed up in a phrase, — exceptional good
sense.   He was the practical man turned
man of letters, never willingly losing contact with the earth.   Therefore his flights
are exhilarating runs, and not excursions
into the air.   He has no quarrel with civilization.   He is a friend to law.   "He
wishes," says Bersot, "in private life, reason dominating feeling, and yielding in its
turn to faith, which is a less wavering support, chastity, love associated with duty in
marriage and in the family; for public life,

duty again, intrusted by preference to law,
but with no infringement of the right without which a man is no longer a man, — the
liberty of the individual, the liberty of conscience.   In politics he believed in the
government of the middle classes, which
represent reason and moderation.   A wholly
practical mind that found no enjoyment whatever in pure fancy, pure poetry, or the speculations of philosophy. . . . He is strong on
the ground of reality and the practical."

But Girardin's practical common-sense
is not of the blunt and blundering kind
that so justly merits ridicule under the name
of Philistinism.   It is united with the rare
tact that is born of perfect understanding.
In argument he is a light skirmisher that
disarms his antagonist by his skill and imperturbable self-possession, before they can
come to heavy blows.   It is impossible to
conceive of two minds so wholly antagonis-
tic as Girardin's and Rousseau's; and while
Girardin is unsparing in his demonstration
of Rousseau's weakness, he is just and even
tender towards him.   You shall smile at
Rousseau's vanity, but you shall not mock
him; you shall pity his frailty, but you shall
not wholly despise him.   In spite of all the

smoke and vapor that obscured the flame, you shall know that there burned in him the immortal light of genius. Only, on the other hand, you shall not take the smoke and vapor for light because they accompany it. You shall know that they are stifling, unwholesome, impure. Rousseau's morbid sensibility, his excessive and irritable vanity, his seductive sophistries are the occasion of some of Girardin's finest criticism.

"Jean Jacques Rousseau," he writes, "is the chief of a school that takes sensibility for the sovereign law of its life. According to this school, whoever allows himself to be guided by his sensibility cannot go astray, or at any rate can err only in a legitimate and honest way. This school believes that the heart of man is good, — grave error. It is not good, it is tender, and tender towards evil as towards good. Mdlle. de Scudéry, in one of the sentimental conversations with which 'Clélie' is full, defines sensibility as 'tenderness of soul.' The definition is not exact. Sensibility depends very much upon the senses. There is a great deal of youthfulness and ardor of blood in it, and those who are remarkable for sensibility at thirty are hard and egoistic at sixty. Besides its moral weakness, there is another objection to sensibility; it is full of illusions, I was almost about to say, full of lies. It deceives man with regard to himself. It makes him believe that he has the strength of good sentiments in having their emotions. Thus deceived on his own part, he easily deceives others, and from dupe becomes charlatan.

"How many emotions are born with heat of blood and pass away with it! And it is this, by the way, which gives to young people their charm and their happy confidence in themselves. They do honor to their soul for the emotions due to their age. Rousseau had this kind of sensibility, at the same time, weak and ardent. It served him in his works, and led him astray in his life. Rousseau had read many romances, and this sort of reading developed the sensibility that began with being a charm and ended with being a disease. . . . For a man of feeling, the worst possible thing is to be his own guide, and to be without a calling that rules his conduct and traces his career in advance, and without a family to serve as a support for him and a barrier against his fancy, or, in default of a family, a firm and enlightened guide. The man of feeling in many respects resembles woman. If he does not receive his destiny ready-made from the hands of his family or those of a good director, he receives it from chance or the sway of his passions. . . .

"Rousseau left Mme. de Warens 'without leaving or scarcely feeling the least regret for a separation, the very thought of which would formerly have given us the anguish of death.' There are your heroes and heroines of sensibility! They think themselves born to live and die together. But let the least accident happen, an annoyance, an absence, and there is immediate indifference and oblivion; inevitable *dénouement* of affections that the soul very inappropriately attributes to herself, but which come from accident and the ardor of youth. This moment of repugnance and separation is a moment that novelists carefully conceal. They make their heroes and heroines die rather than separate them, and they are right. The separations of death are not so sad as those of indifference."

With regard to Rousseau's placing his children in a foundling asylum, Girardin continues: "There, again, you have one of the most characteristic traits of sensibility.

It is incapable of recognizing duty, when
duty appears in the form of an embarrass-
ment or a sacrifice, when it is unaccompa-
nied with a feeling of pleasure. . . . Put no
trust in the morality of a heart that searches
its duties in emotions, and does not believe
man obliged to do his duty but when he is
touched. The idea of duty has this virtue
in it that it resists weariness, distraction,
forgetfulness, and that we feel guilty when
we feel negligent or indifferent. On the
other hand, when obligation seeks sentiments only, it is effaced with the very sentiment which it has created. . . .

"The vices of civilization which Rousseau
enumerates with the most complacency are
the vices and defects of the social world and
of the salons. 'Jealousy, coldness, reserve,
fear, suspicion, hatred, and betrayal,' he
says, 'are continually hidden under this
uniform and perfidious veil of politeness,
under this much boasted urbanity that we
owe to the enlightenment of our century.'
It is easy to see in every word, here, the
souvenirs that Jean Jacques carried away
from the salons in the evening, and the con-
solatory reflections that he made upon himself. He has suffered from the coldness and

reserve that he is astonished at finding associated with politeness in society.   He has
suffered from it, because of his inexperience.
He has mistaken politeness for affection,
and he has wanted to give his soul at first
sight to men who gave him their hand, and
his heart to every woman who bowed to him.
Then, seeing that he was deceived, he has
fallen into suspicion and fear, and he will
fall deeper and deeper into it every day, and
will finish by seeing enemies and traitors
everywhere."

Girardin finds the root of Rousseau's melancholy in vanity deceived.   He quotes
Mme. d'Épinay's observation: "Rousseau is
now nothing in my eyes, but a moral dwarf
mounted on stilts."   "In all ages," Girardin
adds, "the great corruptors are those who
change the good into evil, or the evil into
good; who say that property is theft, marriage is slavery, adultery is liberty."

Girardin has no patience with the melancholy assumed by the disciples of Rousseau,
and their affected nature-worship that turned
nature into the "confidante of their self-
love, the echo of their vanity. . . . Sadness
seemed originality.   They made themselves
melancholy in order to be superior, and hast-

ened to get rid of their illusions before taking time to become experienced." Then he sums up admirably the characteristic features of that false melancholy which is but the result of "sharpened and embittered vanity, the despair which needs to show itself, the melancholy which instead of consuming itself wishes to excite universal pity and admiration, the assumption of the rôle of a martyr instead of that of a simple unfortunate; all of which is so repugnant to the idea of a real and deep grief.

"Rousseau loves humanity, and he cannot endure individuals. . . . Seen from a distance, and viewed as a whole, humanity can be loved without very much trouble. But those who truly love men are they who patiently endure individuals. Without such patient endurance, the love of humanity is an idea that heats the brain; it is not at all an affection that fills the heart."

It is this affectation of noble sentiments and reality of ignoble vanity that makes Rousseau so repugnant to Girardin. "Our friends may have many defects," he writes, "but what I demand of them, above all, is to be true. In loving them, I want to love a man and not a manikin. I want their

language to be real feeling and not mere
rhetoric.   When I shake hands with them,
I want a firm pressure and not a fine gesture.   Now, in Rousseau, the gesture pre-
dominates; the assumed character destroys
the individual."

In the same penetrating way that he un-
masks the ulcered vanity of Rousseau, Girardin uncovers the egotism and dryness of
heart that lie at the bottom of the melancholy of Chateaubriand's famous René:
"This mingling of refined sentiments and
savage tastes, this soul that demands happiness from new scenes and carries about with
it its own wretchedness in itself, — all this
makes of René a character apart, that unfortunately has become one of the general types
of the literature of our day.   If I should try
to define, in brief, the secret of René's misery, I should say that it is inability to love.
The characteristic of souls that are able to
love is to give themselves to those they
love, and to find their joy and satisfaction
in this gift.   For, let us not deceive ourselves, it is not the love we inspire that satisfies the soul, it is that which we feel.   The
soul feels empty when it does not love, and
it can be filled only by the tenderness which

it gives. Hence the anguish of René. He
is astonished at being loved and being neither
calm nor satisfied. He cannot love; that is
his torment. . . . He is a brain and a body,
he is not a soul. His heart has no flames by
which love can be warmed. I grant that he
is seductive; he has imagination, ardor, all
that creates a belief in love, and even this
melancholy and *ennui* that every woman
hopes to dissipate is a charm that attracts
pity and vanity. But the seductiveness lasts
no longer than it takes to discover this fatal
impotence to love which is in his soul. . . .
René is melancholy in a disappointed century; that is why he has so much sadness, for
his melancholy is far from being as original
as he claims it is. Beneath the poetical
melancholy of René I recognize I know not
how many little vexations and petty disap-
pointments of the century; on one side the
lassitude of a conscience wearied with having believed and vexed at being able to believe no longer, disgust with principle, faith
in chance; on the other side, vanity that
loves *éclat*, the mania for display, the taste
for theatrical emotion, and at the bottom of all these vain, egotistic puerilities,
is to be found *ennui*, — that fatal and inevi-

table consequence of all man's attempts to live self-centred. How are these errors of vanity and *ennui* to be rectified? 'There is,' said the old Chactas to René, — 'there is no happiness except in the common ways.' Chactas is right, and that is the moral to be drawn from René's story. Little minds believe that the extraordinary dispels *ennui*, and they become disgusted with the ordinary train of life, and search great adventures, and indulge in grave reveries which become small and foolish as soon as they mingle in them. In this way René and his reveries have become a commonplace, thanks to those features of intimate resemblance that René had with our century, but which he concealed under the poetical lustre given to him by his author, — thanks to the affectations of vulgar souls that think they cease to be vulgar by imitating the extraordinary, not understanding that the worst banality is the banality of the extraordinary."

Girardin loves health, strength, law, and order, as only a physician can who is acquainted with the ravages and ruins of disease and disorder. He never wearies of attacking false sentiments, — that "sadness which comes from the disorder and softness of the soul; the morbid excitability of those who think they belong to the élite because they have not the strength of ordinary souls, — who cultivate their sensibility till they tremble at the slightest touch, to whom every movement is a shock, every scratch a wound, every contradiction a despair; — the soul turned sybarite that cannot bear the crumple of a rose-leaf."

"Genius is patient and long-lived," he cries; "the strength to live is the essential part of it.   Look at Homer, Tasso, Dante, Milton.   They did not escape wretchedness, yet they lived because they had within them the strength to support the pains of life. God did not give them genius like a volatile perfume which evaporates when the flask that contains it is shaken, but he gave it as a generous viaticum to sustain the man during a long voyage.   What! you have within you a divine and immortal thought and you do not know how to support the vexations of life, the disdain of fools, the wickedness of calumniators, the coldness of the indifferent? What! you walk with your head in the skies, and complain because an insect concealed in the grass stings your foot in passing? . . . I distrust the genius that can live only in a

conservatory, and I expect from this miserable plant neither sweet-smelling flowers nor
savory fruits."

Girardin likes, he says, to demonstrate as
much as he is able "the union that exists
between good taste and good morals. . . .
Who can deny that the elevation and greatness of character which art demands have a
moral advantage?   What we must search in
good literature — that which conforms to the
veritable rules of art — is this salutary admiration inspired by the view of the great
and good.   The whole question lies in that.
Literature is not charged simply with exciting us by a description of humanity.   This
description ought to aim at the beautiful for
the purpose of elevating the mind.   It ought
to avoid grimaces and convulsions, and to
shun the ugly to the end that the soul shall
not be corrupted or degraded by vicious impressions. . . . Art ought to speak to the
intelligence alone; it is to the mind only,
that it ought to give pleasure.   If it tries to
move the senses, it degrades itself. . . . The
arts are the language of the soul. . . . And
do not think that the literary education we
receive in modern society always protects
the soul from the vulgar emotions of the

body. . . . There are two classes of men who are capable of preferring the brutal emotions of the circus to the noble illusions of the theatre; — those who have not an intellect sufficiently cultivated, and those who have it too much cultivated.

"We begin with low, coarse emotions, but, alas! we end with them too. Satiety leads us back to brutality. Besides, let us not deceive ourselves; the human heart, if it be not careful, is easily seduced to this side. . . . Even the Greeks, the chosen people of the arts, finished by adopting the gladiatorial combats; . . . but from that moment dramatic art ceased to exist in Greece, and the Roman circus replaced the theatre. . . . When the theatre, in its turn, prefers to depict the sensations of the body instead of the emotions of the soul, it approaches the circus; but it also is punished by a prompt decadence."

Of the weak, sentimental hero of a then popular novel, Girardin writes: "He is not good, which is the capital point. I say that he is not good, because he has neither resolution nor reserve in his affections, and that, however tender and exalted such feelings may be, they do not at all merit the name of goodness.   Good sense and strength are essential elements of goodness.   In my opinion, little justice of feeling added to much weakness by no means makes a good heart. It makes a super-sensitive soul, and may God deliver us from super-sensitive souls! . . . The mistakes of the hero come from softness of heart and character, and for all its titles of sensibility, exaltation, and enthusiasm, such a character is none the less contemptible.   All these souls and hearts expand as foam does, and like foam are empty. . . . Imagine a very young man with a face that says, 'Love me,' an air of grace, abandonment, and deathlike languor; eyes filled with vague desires; thin, delicate lips, as fit for the expression of irony as of tenderness; a supple figure; movements that charm, now by their effeminacy, and now by their ease: give to this young man an imagination that embraces everything; give him curiosity rather than ardor in his passions, the talent of reflecting on his emotions rather than feeling them, a capricious and mobile will, a feverish and palpitating nature capable of trembling rather than of being deeply moved, a soul that vibrates and resounds like a musical instrument that is the more sonorous

the hollower it is; — given all this and you
will have the character of the young man
as formed by the customs of society, the
leisure, elegances, and all the habits that
accompany wealth, as well as by the influences of a purely literary and poetical
education. . . . Suicide is the natural and
necessary *dénouement* of a life so badly conducted as his.

"Never having known how to content and
regulate his emotions, it is quite natural
that he should renounce life. Faithfully
representing our epoch, floating like it in
the wind of all the doctrines, our hero,
Henri Farel, also represents by his death
this epoch in which so many young people
renounce life having scarcely tasted it, —
wearied by the first step, because, in place of
principles and beliefs to sustain them, they
have but illusions and the ardor of youth.
When this intoxicating gas that comes from
youthful blood evaporates with age, the poor
balloon falls empty and flat to the ground,
never to rise again."

There is a singular confirmation of the
truth of Girardin's statement concerning the
enervating effects of a purely literary and
poetical education to be found in one of

Lombroso's latest works. The Italian scientist says : "No mathematician, no naturalist that I know of, at least of the very first order, has come under the penalty of a common crime. Nor is there anything strange in this. Men accustomed to breathe the serene atmosphere of science which furnishes scope and delight in itself, men trained to a critical appreciation of the true, more easily succeed in restraining brutal passions, and are naturally repelled by the sterile and tortuous life of crime.

"Literature and art present a less favorable aspect. In many artists and *littérateurs* the passions prevailing more largely, because they are more potent factors of genius, are less restrained by criterions of truth and the severe deductions of logic, and hence are to be found among delinquents : Rousseau, Bonfodio, Aretino, Ceresa, Brunetto Latini, Franco, Foscolo, and perhaps Byron, not to speak of ancient times and barbarous countries when brigandage and poetry went hand in hand, as witness the poems of Kaleiva Peag and Helmbrecht.

"This fact is an important one in connection with the education of the young. It warns us to avoid a training too exclusively rhetorical. Let science and mathematics have their due share of attention. Encourage young men to take up a trade rather than a profession, in order to diminish that great class of idlers who are a perpetual menace to society."

The same infallible good sense which leads Girardin to put his finger on the cause of the weakness of the young men of his generation, leads him to distinguish clearly between the enthusiasms of temperament and the enthusiasms of experienced judgment, between the apparent strength which an absorbing emotion lends to the soul and the real strength which is founded on the calmer emotions of reason. "Since love animates and heats the soul," he writes, "it is quite natural for the soul to mistake the increase of life which it feels for an increase of force, and to believe itself exalted. But it is an error. Love does not change souls; it does not make the bad soul good; it simply makes the good better. One is in love what he is in everything else, — gentle, if he is gentle, ardent, if he is ardent, only a little more so. He is not something other than himself, but he is a little more than himself. Love is a state of the mind in which our faculties without changing their nature change their degree, and increase or are excited by a sort of instinctive commotion. . . . Lovers are not generous, devoted, disinterested, virtuous, but towards one another. They are not so towards the rest of the world. Their virtue is a secret between them. Their neighbor knows nothing of it. Now, there are no virtues that are not in some degree virtues towards everybody. The virtues which have an object so particular and a circle so limited are feelings, not virtues. Such is love. It inspires devotion, but towards whom? Towards the person we love, that is to say, towards ourselves. A man saves his mistress from peril because he loves her, but he does not devote himself to his country or to his religion because he loves his mistress. . . . The raptures of passion pass for qualities in the doctrine of romance; the confessions and thoughtless effusions of love are the signs of a beautiful soul, and are very nearly regarded as good actions. . . . Shop-clerks and students have elevated the passions or instincts of their age, its generous sentiments, into sacred enthusiasms. They have believed themselves innocent in debauchery because they were ardent in it.

The *grisettes*, in their turn, have believed themselves heroines of tenderness, until some fine day this sentimental dupery or charlatanry yields to the fate of all false sentiments which inevitably end in gross emotions or sordid calculations. The Platos of the counting-house and the mansards are changed without much difficulty into Epicures: '*Epicuri de grege porci.*'"

"Love," says Girardin elsewhere, — "love in modern and even in contemporaneous literature which so often imitates what it criticises, — love holds the first place. The ancients are fathers, husbands, sons, citizens, — all, in short, that men can be. The moderns, to believe the poets and novelists, are nothing but lovers; and of the four divisions of human life, infancy, youth, maturity, and old age, there is but one, youth, which literature chooses to depict. The age that the novelist assigns to his characters, and — shall I say it too? — the age at which the majority of novelists begin to write, prevents the affections which make the strength and joy of the family from being represented in a great and strong manner. In fact, respect for these affections is not learned until late. There comes, I know, a day in which lovers play the part of husbands, or sons the part of fathers; but novels, in general, are arranged to end that day. They lead their heroes to the family, but quit them on the threshold.

"In Walter Scott's novels love does not hold the first place. It is sometimes the subject of a tale, but even then it does not make the principal theme. The sentiments of father and son, mother and wife, brother and sister, citizen and stranger, victor and vanquished, the peculiar manners of an epoch, — this is what Scott represents instead of depicting the infinite vicissitudes of a single passion."

Elsewhere Girardin pays a fine tribute to Scott for his gift of seeing the good side of human nature, and his determination "even in his description of beggars, Bohemians, contrabands, not to pique the curiosity of the idlers in high society by painting this lower world in its grossness, its ugliness, its brutal pleasures, and its ignoble language, but to search behind the rags and in the slang for the elevated sentiment, the noble and touching word, that belongs to all men, whatever their rank, but which is not found except at the moment when the soul rises to the level of action.

"Scott has in a supreme degree this benevolent clairvoyance, this intuition of the beautiful and good through the shadows of the human soul, through the inequalities of social condition; and this, to my mind, makes the charm and moral merit of his novels. But he is not of the school that lends to crime an insolent grandeur or corrupt seduction; he does not make heroes of criminals. . . . Vice is often sentimental and melancholy; it interests and touches the heart under the pretext of guarding still in its abasement something great and good. In short, it seems that we have a taste for ruins in morals as well as in architecture, that we like better what is half fallen than what stands upright. Let us love, I agree to it, what is still pure in perverted souls, as a testimony to human dignity that is never wholly lost; but let us not admire the ruin except in memory of the edifice; let us not esteem the rag more highly than the material in good condition. In short, let us not take in criminals what remains of virtue as an excuse, and let us not push the pity inspired by the excuse so far as respect and admiration."

That which has nothing but its novelty to

commend it finds no favor with Girardin. He is enamoured of the grand commonplaces, — the face of earth and sky in nature, and in literature the old truths of human experience. "The commonplace," he says, "is the immemorial rendezvous of all minds. Everybody agrees to it; it makes law; it makes proverbs. Turn it into fiction or into story and immediately it takes possession of all minds. It seizes the whole man, — his imagination and his reason. . . . The secret of poetry is but to say better than anybody else what everybody thinks. . . . Great poets and great orators do nothing but give, by the force of their expression, a particular accent to a commonplace."

In the same vigorous way in which he attacks false sentiment, Girardin attacks the thoughtless revolutionary spirit of youth, and the belief that political institutions are responsible for individual wretchedness, crime, and poverty.

"Everybody," he says, "is a revolutionist at twenty. Some begin to lose their heat at twenty-five, but the majority push their ardor to thirty, and to the time of their marriage. The revolutionary spirit, even in the most ardent, hardly continues beyond the nursing of the first child, and ceases with its weaning."

Marriage with its duties and responsibilities, its practical teaching of the interdependence of human beings, lessens, according to Girardin, the wish to take risks in foolhardy experiments. It teaches, too, that a man's destiny is not the plaything of social institutions, but the work of his own hands.

"Take away pride and envy from the heart of man," he continues, "and what remains of the revolutionary spirit? Nothing or almost nothing, — a few hollow maxims, some obscure sentences, and some principles that admit of all sorts of interpretations. For the past four years" [written in 1852] "we have heard a great deal about socialism, and we have been very near seeing its works. As a doctrine, socialism is the most pitiable thing in the world. Nothing is so vague and confused. What is it, then, that makes the strength and the danger of socialism? The evil sentiments of the human heart. Socialism makes proselytes only after corrupting souls. Socialism, with its infinite contradictions, is a veritable tower of Babel, that is to say, an impossibility. But it is a tower of Babel having for its garrison the seven deadly sins, and that makes its strength."

Writing of the proneness of incapacity and envious idleness to shift the responsibility of their miserable condition from their own shoulders to those of society, Girardin says : —

"In our day there is another mysterious but less guilty being besides destiny, whom we willingly accuse of our misfortunes. Her name is society. How many the complaints against her! how many the maledictions! Archias was born poor. That certainly is the fault of destiny. But as Archias is neither active nor industrious, he stays poor, and then accuses society of his poverty. 'This society,' he says, 'is badly organized, — no justice, no equity. Everything goes contrary to good sense.' What is necessary, then, in order that Archias shall find society well organized? He must be rich and idle in it. It is at this price only that he will declare that a revolution is no longer necessary. The revolution that elevates him ought to be the last, because it is the only just and legitimate one. . . . He has a complete plan of reform for society, and its fun-

damental principle is to set up what is down
and pull down what is up, — and all that in
the name of the rights of man and the progress of civilization.

"The essential character of the revolutionary spirit is the belief that in sup-
pressing such and such an institution, in
overthrowing such and such a dynasty, we
shall suppress evil in society. By no means!
You change the laws and the government,
but do you at the same time change your
vices into virtues? Do you become wiser,
more scrupulous, more honest? Do you
renounce your errors and your prejudices?
That is the revolution that has never been
tried, and which deserves trying, — a revolution which would be the improvement or
conversion of each one of us. I am inclined
to believe that in proportion as individuals
become of more worth, society will grow
better. For the last sixty years we have
been trying to solve a very difficult problem,
— that is, to make a good whole out of bad
constituents, — to found a city of God on the
seven capital sins. There lies the fundamental error of the revolutionary spirit. It
desires to create a perfect government, and
it commences by giving a loose rein to the

vices of the human heart.   It takes the road
to hell to go to Paradise, and it is surprised
to find itself still on the way. . . .   In our
day there is no social inequality but difference in education.   I am not chimerical
enough to believe that this inequality can be
abolished, but I am persuaded that it can be
diminished, and that it is the duty of every
good citizen to work at the lessening of the
distance that separates high society from
that below.   I believe that true Christian
charity demands it, and that liberal politics
requires it.   The day in which there will be
some common literary pleasure between the
laboring and the lettered classes, — the day
on which we shall read together some scenes
from Corneille and Racine, some of La Fontaine's fables, some pages of Bossuet, — the
day on which we shall be penetrated in common, if but for a moment, by the light of
beauty and the warmth of goodness, — that
day political and social prejudices will be
effaced, and many rancors of jealousy will
disappear.

"We complain that luxury is spreading
among the lower classes, and with reason,
because the enjoyments of luxury are to all
classes the cause of jealousy and rivalry.

Literary enjoyment, which is a luxury also, is, on the contrary, a cause of union. It is shared, as light is shared, without diminution of one part at the expense of another."

The same good judgment, clearness, and acuteness that characterize Girardin's literary criticism are to be found in all his utterances on educational questions. In his opinion, "the greatest eulogy that can be pronounced on a man is to say that he knows how to get out of a difficulty, — not only to get out of a difficulty by a clever speech in an assembly, a witty and amiable conversation in a salon, a good plea in a law-suit, a just appreciation of the chances of loss or gain in a business speculation, — not to be able to get out of a difficulty by his wit and intelligence alone, but by the skill of his hands if need be, — not only to get out of a difficulty in great things but in little ones, — not to be in constant need of having his arms linked in those of other people, not to be embarrassed either by his person or his belongings, — to have the wit of expediency and activity, — to be neither awkward nor soft, — to know how to live, in short, without a bell under his fingers and a servant at the end of the bell."

The whole man educated, hand, heart, brain, — independence, cheerfulness, indomitable endurance, resolute will developed in him, — this is Girardin's ideal; and he knows that it is not to be attained by weak indulgence, that you can't teach a child to walk by carrying him in your arms, that you must set him on the ground, let him fall and rise again, and not be too fearful about the bumps he gets in consequence   To have his pleasure only in view, to shield him always from crosses and vexations, is to render him incapable of meeting the responsibilities or enduring the trials of life.   For this reason Girardin does not believe that study should be converted into play, — that kindergarten methods should follow the youth into the grammar school and high school, because the suppression of all difficulty in study is the suppression of its greatest utility.

"Amused children," he says, "are generally melancholy and discontented young people."   He thinks that education should give an impulse to unceasing growth, and yet, "how many men," he adds, "stop growing at twenty-five and always remain 'promising youths,' just as many young men have already become and will always remain

'children of whom much is hoped.' How
many degrees there are in human life, and
how few are they who pass through them all!
There are no great men but those who unceasingly grow greater, who add the progress of youth to that of infancy; the progress
of maturity to that of youth, and who like
vigorous oaks are crowned but in extreme
old age. But how few there are among men
who have this living sap in them, and to
whom each year brings a new leaf and every
age a new strength!"

The practical training which he finds
necessary for a man, Girardin wishes also
for woman. "Dancing and music are not
for every day, and especially not for every
moment." He is not, however, a believer
in what is called the enfranchisement of
women. In his opinion, "woman was created to belong to a master whom she possesses," and finds her destiny fulfilled and
her happiness assured only in marriage.
However ugly this dictum of master and
ownership may sound in feminine ears, Girardin is by no means wanting in the greatest respect and honor for woman, and he
makes that respect and honor the symbol of
civilization. "In whatever country you may

be," he writes, "wherever you see woman honored and respected, you are in a civilized country. They tell me that in the United States a woman can go from one end of that vast republic to another, passing through half-built towns and half-cleared forests, and everywhere, on the railroads, in the taverns, the steamboats, she meets nothing but honor and respect. By that sign I believe in the future of the United States; and to persuade me of the greatness of her future, don't talk to me of American commerce, her agriculture, the rapid increase of her population, nor of her towns that rise like magic, nor of North America traversed in all its breadth from New York to San Francisco, nor of the bravery and boldness of her citizens, nor of their wealth and prosperity, — tell me only that a young girl can go from North to South, from East to West, as if she were everywhere under her mother's eye, and I am certain that there is in that country a great and strong civilization."

The most important of Girardin's works are "Literary and Moral Essays," "Life and Works of Jean Jacques Rousseau," "Description of French Literature, followed by a Study of the Literature of the Middle Age of the Renaissance," "La Fontaine and the Fabulists," "Lectures on Dramatic Literature, or the Employment of the Passions in the Drama." The aim of this last work is to show how the expression of sentiment has changed in the course of time, being at first simple and true, then elegant and refined, and later, exaggerated and becoming gross under pretext of returning to the true.

As a critic, Girardin does not rank with Sainte-Beuve, Lessing, and De Quincey. Not only the exigencies of his professional duties, but the very character of his intellect gave him an almost absorbing predilection for the real, — for what can be vigorously touched and handled in the dry, white light of reason. To the twilight truths, felt by intuition and inexplicable by logic, to the subtle and evanescent charms of poetry, he was almost, if not quite, a stranger. Of every truth and every emotion that concerns human life, he asked, "Can I live best and happiest by it?" and if the answer was no, he was inclined to doubt the necessity of its existence. But all his limitations leaned to virtue's side. They were the limitations that belong to perfect sanity, perfect health of mind and body. To be sure, he had felt

in his youth all the overflow of animal spirits that break out in wild pranks or thoughtless disorder, but he had outgrown his
temperamental ardor at the proper time, and
had learned to recognize it for what it was
worth. He had put forth leaf after leaf in
the manner of the man with living sap in
him, whose ceaseless growth he eulogizes.
He had attained the poise that comes from
the healthy activity of all the faculties; and
of the strength that was in him, he not only
gave to others, but he gave them the secret
of it. That is why he has an assured and
honorable, if not the highest, place in criticism. His work is not to increase but to
decrease sensibility, or to turn it into proper
channels. He is the most indefatigable and
successful of chimera-hunters. He frees the
mind from false sentiments to make room for
true ones. His work is akin to that of the
farmer on one of our broad prairies; and if in
his ploughing some fragile and beautiful wild
flower is uprooted, we shall not account it
an unpardonable sin in him, when we gather
the rich harvests of autumn.

V.

XIMÉNES DOUDAN.

CONCEIVE of a nature in almost every particular the contrary of that of Saint-Marc Girardin. For the robust physique and sanguine temperament of the latter, substitute the thinness and suppleness that belong to the nervous, intellectual type, and give to this fragile man of middle stature the sufferings of hypochondria and the morbid imagination that accompanies it. But at the same time add, as a counterbalance, the most exquisite refinement, the most penetrating judgment, lightning flashes of wit, and the lambent play of the kindliest humor, and instead of a dejected invalid and a damp-weather influence you shall have a "man of the most delicate taste, of the brightest mind, and most piquant conversation," the life and soul of a salon, the subtlest of critics, the "oracle of doubtful thoughts" among his friends, — you will have, in short, Ximénes Doudan.

M. Doudan was born in 1800 at Douai, and died at Paris in 1872. An orphan from his earliest childhood, he knew no home-ties, and was singularly reticent regarding himself, never speaking of his past nor of his family. His education was completed at Paris, where he was still living in obscurity in 1826, but already noted among his youthful associates as a young man of extraordinary promise. Among his friends was Saint-Marc Girardin, who recommended him to the critic Villemain, who in turn introduced him to the Duc de Broglie, son-in-law of Mme. de Staël.

The Duc de Broglie was looking for a tutor for the son of Mme. de Staël left from her marriage with M. de Rocca. Entering the family as tutor, Doudan's sterling qualities soon made him a trusted and honored member of it. At the death of Monsieur le Duc, Doudan continued in the household of the Duchesse, and for nearly forty years was the life of the salon in the Hôtel de Broglie.

He lived a simple, uniform life, remote from public action, but in rapport with political matters. He read incessantly. His taste was early matured by familiarity with the Greek and Roman classics, among whom

his favorites were Homer, Plato, Virgil, and
Tacitus. But with all his love for the ancients, he was by no means indifferent to
the moderns, and read everything that appeared. Beyond a few articles contributed
to the "Journal des Débats," and the "Revue Française," Doudan published nothing.
During his lifetime his reputation was that
of a brilliant talker and an incomparable
letter-writer, a kind of reputation whose
merits are but hearsay to the general public.

The public learned the secret of this reputation when, after Doudan's death, a volume
of his selected correspondence appeared, followed by a thin volume of detached thoughts
entitled "Maximes et Pensées."

French literature is particularly rich in
Memoirs, Confessions, and Correspondences,
and though other literatures may boast of
their biographical and autobiographical masterpieces, — their Boswells and Cellinis and
Jung Stillings, there has been but one
Mme. de Sévigné. As letter-writers, the
French are incomparably the masters of us
all. They have in perfection the art of saying nothings in not only the most acceptable
but the most exquisite way. Out of a dull
little commonplace fact you shall have food

for mirth or food for fancy, — a grotesque face carved in a cherry-stone, or a breath and a drop of water transformed into a filmy, floating sphere that catches the light and throws it back to you in radiant colors.

The true letter-writer is one of those amiable egotists, like La Fontaine or Charles Lamb, who delight you the more they speak of their tastes, their temper, and their idiosyncrasies. Their letters are changing portraits of themselves; you see them, now in this attitude, now in that, and no attitude is a pose, but a careless and natural falling into the positions that varied activity requires. The true letter is a conversation of the best kind; that is, it presupposes not only a good listener, but one who is ready to give as well as to take. You can't be witty with a fence-post. You need to know that you speak to an intelligence that answers your own, and by its vigorous reaction renders you again the force that you gave. Like a conversation, it admits, too, of the greatest variety of theme and movement. It leaps, it runs, it skims lightly over the surface, it pauses here and there for a vigorous thrust and then on again. The one thing it is in duty bound not to do is to set you to yawning, and everything is admissible in it that serves this end, even if it be but the teasing sophistry that wakes you to its vigorous denial.

As a letter-writer, Doudan answers all the demands that can be made of him and more. His letters abound in judgments so acute on the literature and politics of his day that they have a value beyond that of mere entertainment, and entitle him to a high rank among the critics of his time. "Good sense, good taste, acuteness, and imagination make of him an exquisite critic," says Scherer. "Sometimes this criticism is but a sentence, but it is a sentence that engraves."

Unfortunately, Doudan belonged to that sensitive and fastidious type of intellectual men whose worship of the ideal results in a partial paralysis of their power. Amiel, Joubert, and the English poet Thomas Gray, are of this type. They are men of contemplation rather than of action, — men enamoured of perfection and satisfied with nothing less, who, discouraged at the distance between their achievements and their ideals, pass their lives in a painful struggle between the desire to produce and the consciousness of impotence to reach the standard they have raised for themselves. Such men leave us but a scanty testimony to their powers, but it is finished, it is exquisite in its quality. They do their best work in that friendly intimacy in which the mind, forgetful of the ideal which is almost its bugbear, works freely and easily, following simply the dictates of its own individuality. They are inimitable talkers and inimitable letter-writers. There are a few of Joubert's letters that are worth all his "Pensées," and the same may be said of Doudan. His letters have an ease, a vivacity, a quaint turn of imagery entirely wanting in the more labored productions of the volume entitled "Maximes et Pensées." In searching for a soberer expression of his thoughts for the public, he robs them of the color, the natural grace, and force they have when they come warm from his mind and overflow into his letters.

Therefore it is from Doudan's letters that we shall make the extracts necessary to illustrate the peculiar quality of his intellect; and, to begin with, let us note the fine balance of his mind preserved amidst the distractions of a delicate frame, subject to all sorts of nervous disorders. The preserva-

tion of a like poise is not common enough
to pass without remark. It is the testimony
to an intellect finely cultivated and rich in
resources, — an intellect that can make its
own happiness without the aid of exterior
helps. Narrow minds fill and overflow with
the worries and anxieties of life, and suc-
cumb entirely to physical maladies. They
can see life fair, only when all is fair without them, and their digestion and circula-
tion are unimpaired. In the see-saw of their
fluctuating emotions, they are optimists or
pessimists according as their pulse runs high
or low. They never disentangle the real and
permanent from the accidental and transitory, and the stream of their life is not the
full, broad, onward sweep that carries with
it pebble and leaf and fallen tree-trunk, and
receives its tributaries on every hand; on
the contrary, it is turned aside by every tiny
obstruction it meets, and loses itself continually in countless little rills that end at last
in stagnant pools.

Doudan was not vitally attacked, but he
suffered all his life from the most irritating
of maladies, — that of sick nerves. "With
an imagination a little morbid," he writes,
"one has some difficulty in subjecting him-

self to the rule of strict reason. I am in part really sick, and I have restless and mutinous nerves. The result is, I do not do half what I want to do, and three-fourths of the time I do not say half what I mean."

He had the nervous organization of an hysterical woman, and it was only the man's intellect and resolute will in him that kept him from shattering to pieces. He had frequent attacks of violent headache that are none the less to be regarded an evil because one does not die of them, as he somewhere remarks. He suffered frequently from that nervous exhaustion in which the mind shares the hopeless weariness of the body, and expresses it in the mute misery of an utter extinction of all the interests of life. "Then you know, too," he writes to a friend, "this odious malady of fatigue. It is certainly an invention of the devil, who, knowing that activity is the great remedy for all the ills, has devised a trick which turns out to be this inconvenience from which we suffer. If this kind of chronic weariness were like the fatigue after a long walk, we should have the pleasure of repose, but generally this exhaustion is mingled with nervous irritation. I am not sure that the souls of Brutus and

Cato, wholly stoical as they were, could have resisted this kind of captivity; but very likely the ancients were not acquainted with these nervous disorders, and the devil had not yet made his discovery." Elsewhere he says : "I am continually in a wretchedly nervous condition. All my physicians say that nothing is the matter with me. My good sense also tells me that, but I am none the less taken captive by my dragons whenever I am alone. . . . It is clear that I have always had an intensely nervous temperament, — the temperament which makes the spasmodic, hysterical, and epileptic, but I have never yielded to these extravagances. I have an obstinate sore throat of which there is no external sign, and which the doctor says is spasmodic."

"I have never yielded to any of these extravagances." In that assertion lies the secret of the strength of the man. He had a powerful will; his mind was no party to the weaknesses of his body. It sat in judgment on them, pronounced them what they were, and refused their domination. He contented himself with feeling his pulse; he did not record, as Amiel did, the various moods dependent on the swiftness or slowness of its beats.   Beyond the allusions we have quoted, his letters contain no hint of hypochondria.   On the contrary, they are uniformly cheerful, and move in a sphere out of the reach of physical ailments.   He even gayly transforms the need of repose he feels, and the enforced rests he takes, into a good and not an evil.

"You complain," he writes to a friend, "of the effects of the great and wise rest you are taking.   You think you are not making noise enough.   There are moments of intellectual drouth similar to those felt by pious persons in religious matters.   It is the moment when the wings are silently growing again.   Continual activity degrades thought more than those grand silences during which it is regaining its strength.   Look at the busy people who are always in action.   Little by little they grow dry and superficial. Every morning they sow a poor hastily growing little plant that is mowed in the evening. There are neither great oaks nor deep lakes in these plains.

"What could the Wandering Jew know of all the sights that had passed under his eye? Where he saw the swallows come, he could not see them leave.   The noise of his foot-

steps prevented him from hearing the silence
of night. If he entered a town that was up
in arms, he vainly returned to see which had
been victorious, the tyrant or the oppressed.
Thus continual activity cuts the thread of
thought. The moments in which we think
we vegetate in a useless repose are those in
which the soul hovers over abysses or over
heights to bring back treasures of whose existence she had no suspicion."

Even when his eyes fail him, and he can
neither read nor bear the light of day, he
does not break out into querulous complaint.
He simply says that there are some maladies
that can be conquered by resistance, but that
this malady of the eyes is not one of them,
— that not to be able to read at all is a terrible trial, and that nothing less resembles
reading than being read to.

Perhaps this delicate, sensitive frame,
more susceptible than most to the jars of
life, might have been rendered more robust
by a less sedentary life, — a life in which
daylight and not gaslight shone on him
oftener, — but he was social by instinct. He
loved good conversation, and he liked to
escape from himself. In this he differed
from the purely contemplative spirits like

Amiel, as he differed from them also in giving color and wings to his seriousness instead of clothing her in sombre hues and clogging her with weights. It was his social experience that taught him how to be arch in his gravity and smilingly ironical even in his indignation, as when he writes of Louis Napoleon: "He seems to be possessed with the fury of being Emperor of something or somebody. He is stubborn as a wild ass. (I speak politely for fear that he may one day be my master.) I believe that he is exceedingly stupid. It is not uncommon to be stupid, but it is uncommon to be stubborn in France. Blessed are they who are stubborn, for they shall possess the earth. To him who wishes to enter a house, there comes a moment, if he knock at the door every five minutes, when the half-open door will yield. It remains to be seen what will be done on his entrance. I hope he may be put out by the shoulders, but it won't be done without devastation."

Doudan had that imaginative vigor which most naturally expresses itself in fresh and lively similes and metaphors. He was an etcher with words. He could seize the telling points of a character or an incident in a few bold strokes, as when he writes of Abraham Lincoln: "The democrats will do well to guard his memory preciously, for he is the finest portrait of their race. He is exactly the ideal democrat, — simple, rugged, mild, patient, courageous when the primitive sentiments of human nature lay hold of him by the throat. Pericles did not speak so well of the young Athenians who died in the Peloponnesian war as he did over the American dead brought home to the great desolate cemetery near the city of Washington."

Doudan liked color in style. "You are a lover of gray tints," he writes to M. Raulin. "According to you, to be a poet is to be sober. If the earth were to be made over again, you would put only swans and geese on it, — all white birds, no scarlet flamingos, no colibris, no fireflies, and you would make the sun set in a great white-sheeted bed, with white curtains and a white nightcap. A pretty king of day, by my faith! Know, sir, that at the bottom of this theory of soberness lies hidden a cold poison that slowly kills the imagination. Soberness is a limit and not a motive. You make it a motive. You abstain from drinking for the mere pleasure of saying, 'I have not drunk.'

Well, what of it? If you did not drink for five hundred years, what would your régime do for the progress of intelligence? The apostle says that we ought to think soberly, *sapere ad sobrietatem.* It is a rule of æsthetics also. . . . You enjoy so vividly the pleasure of not seeing color, of not hearing noises that are too loud, of not encountering a brusque movement, that the foundation of your system is: *Je ne vois que la nuit, n'entends que le silence,* I see but the night, hear but the silence."

Yet Doudan's love of color was not without limitation. He disliked, as much as those of severer taste, all extravagance in the use of it, and the gaudy rhetoric of Hugo and Taine displeased him excessively. Writing of the latter apropos of an article in the "Revue des deux Mondes," he says: "Taine has written three pretty pages in the last number on Leonardo; but how red, blue, green, ivory-black, mother-of-pearl, opal, iris, and purple they are! His article is a dye-merchant's shop. One might say of it with the elder Mirabeau, 'Quel tapage de couleur!'" and of Hugo: "He is a gigantic blusterer who preaches the clemencies of philanthropy with the accent of 1793. . . .

He has written some charming verses mingled with the strangest balderdash. Beside
an old slipper and broken pots, you come
suddenly upon a beautiful wild rose wet with
dew. In my opinion, he mixes everything
in this way without premeditated design.
He does not distinguish the beautiful from
the ugly. He has a powerful enough nature,
which produces with vigor and indifference
palms, serpents, toads, humming-birds, and
spiders. He puts them all into a sack and
there is a volume done."

A score of pages could not convey with
more vigor and precision a juster idea of
Hugo's defects than these few lines. Yet
there was that in the nature of Doudan's
imagination which made him peculiarly susceptible to the charms of romance. Unlike
Saint-Marc Girardin, the world of reality
was not the only world to him. Without
being in any sense a mystic, he knew something of the pleasure of those excursions
into the land of shadows and darkness from
which, if one brings back no definite idea of
particular objects, he brings back at least
a general sense of vastness and profundity,
and a humbling consciousness that there is
a reality beyond the reality that we can see

and lay hold of.   Speaking of a French treatise on German philosophy, he says with Ampère: "I like better those great troubled marshes deep in places, than these two or three glasses of clear water which the French genius throws into the air with a certain force, flattering himself in the mean time that he is going as high as the nature of things."

For the same reason, Renan's rationalism was particularly repulsive to him.   "He is a great *coquet* in the rank of theologians and savants," he writes of Renan.   "His coquetry is mingled with impertinence, but he gives to the men of his generation exactly what they want, — *bonbons* that savor of the infinite.   He is like those chemists who have made a very agreeable drink of cod-liver oil; only the active principles have vanished with the cod-liver, and children are as consumptive as ever.   He irritates me by obliging me to take what he says for reasoning, and — not to drop the subject — have you ever asked yourself why women in particular almost always make conversation turn upon music?   I fancy it is because music, though superior to all the arts, even literature, in the power of speaking to the

soul where words fail us, has the inherent
defect of being very vague and of being half
sensuous, half moral in an extreme degree.
It loves to be excited more than to reflect.
It wishes to enjoy everything without making a virile effort at reconciliation. It rocks
itself in music as in a swing, now high, now
low, without ever advancing, or ever exercising volition. Renan, too, with his sweet,
dreamy, insinuating style winding around
questions without pressing them hard, after
the manner of tiny snakes, gives to his readers the intoxication of the swing. His music
is a boudoir music like that which Plato condemned in the education of youth. It is to
the sound of such music that we resign ourselves to being entertained by everything,
— that we support despotism while dreaming of liberty, — that we forget to row, giving ourselves up to the insensible currents
of the water, while pleasantly dreaming of
those energetic souls who in an earlier day
so transformed and improved the world, —
saying in our insolent pride: 'These souls
were narrow, and did not understand the
world's complexity.'"

Doudan loved the ideal, but he loved it in
due proportion, animated by reality, which

he called the seedling on which the ideal is to be grafted, lest it quickly decay. "I am in a rage," he writes, "with those well-made intellects that have no taste but for the real. Let men once grow insensible to the romantic pleasures of the imagination within the reach of all, and nothing is left them to do but to seek after riches, because riches give conventional pleasures that are within the reach of the lowest imaginations. He who cannot people a cell with the luxury of his dreams will inhabit a palace in vain. He will be as stupid there as the dazzling upholstery that surrounds him. I am astonished that the English poet who wrote the 'Pleasures of the Imagination,' did not see that he might have made a useful book, and reconciled almost everybody to the mediocrity of his situation by showing him the poetic side of everything. I mean by that the point by which the particular order is attached to the universal order. He who is accustomed to live in this contemplation, which is not difficult, will not only be sufficiently happy because his wants will be few, but he will also be wise and lovable. It is in this sense that M. Ampère, the geometrician, said: 'I believe that the exterior world was created to give us an opportunity to think,' — that is to say, to dream and to try to transform what is about us into the image of the truly beautiful as it exists in the ideal. If I were a clergyman, I should preach on this theme, and the peasants would find happiness in the sunshine that streams through their windows. . . . It is very possible that in our day the devil inhabits the world in the form of utility. He has maliciously thought that this is the worst trick that can be played on the beautiful. . . . The wish to be well fed, well clothed, well and rapidly transported makes us lead a very fatiguing life, leaving neither repose to the body nor development to the mind. The world moves, but it is not God that moves it for the quarter of an hour. It moves, but it moves like dogs that turn round and round in order to lie down more comfortably."

The invasion of uncompromising reality into the realm of letters was as distasteful to him as its absorption of life, and in various letters from which the following extracts are taken, he expresses that distaste, now in the form of a protest against the character of the material chosen, the rejection of what is fine and noble in human nature for what is

coarse and low, and again, protesting against
the excessive use of description in the details of material objects.

"Cicero, who was not more romantic than
his age, says somewhere: 'The tree which
the poet plants lives longer than that which
the laborer planted on the edge of his field.'
It might be said that the poets and the novelists of the present age are no longer familiar with these words.   The beings created
by modern imagination have as transitory a
life as that of the Parisian bourgeois.   They
are true enough, but they are the bourgeois
of the imaginative world.   They lack for
their preservation the aromatic spice of the
ideal mingled in a certain proportion with
the real.   But the ideal is the grain of salt
on the bird's tail; if we put on too much,
we make poor Academicians; and if we don't
put on enough, we have but a mortal creature
who dies in the course of a generation. . . .

"When you have finished Lord Byron will
you read *ce chien de livre* that is called
'Mme. Bovary'?   It is not of the same species of literature.   I don't see how young
people nowadays can have the taste to think
that beautiful.   I do not know whether or
not the police-courts ought to condemn it,

but it would have made Racine and Voltaire
sick at their stomach.   The reflection of
filth in the stagnant foulness of a street-
gutter cannot make a fine picture.   Voltaire
drolly remarked that although everything
that is natural was to be found in him, too,
he thought it unseemly to exhibit it all.   I
do not believe that we are in decadence, as it
is said, for the human intellect has made
some new and very valuable acquisitions
during the past fifty years.   But we are in
that disagreeable, wilful age of growth in
which children behave like monkeys. . . .

" Half of our modern æsthetics is an affair
of sympathy with the opinion of others,
and the pliant characters are those that are
thought to have the best taste.   Are n't
there a great many people who think and
admire as others do out of fear of displeasing them?   We do not venture to have our
own opinions except when we are either sure
of pleasing by them or are indifferent about
displeasing. . . .

" To the ancient writer, a table and half a
dozen chairs were all the necessary expendi-
tures for their heroes.   Nowadays we go to
a frightful expense of flowers, trees, arms,
parks, farms, dogs, and forests where the

sage botanist is always ready to be of service to the reveries of each character. . . . Not that I blame all this necessity for painting exteriors, only these fine descriptions ought not to environ a dry mummy, cold, immovable except when made to dance awkwardly by means of a string. . . . At present we like detailed descriptions; we like to see the places that are inhabited by those whose adventures are recounted, — the furniture of their apartments, their gardens, their servants; — in a word, all the externals of their life.' Such descriptions feed the curiosity of languid souls and the passions of our age, which is avid of exterior pleasures simply because there is no strength in its feelings and no pronounced inclinations in its understanding. We seek indomitable passion because our languor can be shaken by nothing less than exaggerated pictures. To this love of exaggerated effects must be added that of sanguinary analyses in which the most delicate and secret fibres are nakedly exhibited; very likely because we love to find the good in evil and the evil in good, and this singular combination is probably to be seen at the bottom of all human dissection. . . .

"If a young buffalo in the Pontine marshes were to write his memoirs, the details of his loves, his jealousies, disorders, and despairs, he would doubtless put into them the same delicacy and the same moral sentiment of good and evil to be found among the buffaloes of his acquaintance; but in proportion as he was a buffalo with a good and cultivated mind, he would not push the descriptive *genre* to these ridiculous excesses. The very sincerity of his passions would prevent him from seeing a multitude of things that did not concern them. While pointing his horns for the combat, he would n't describe to us the little wild flower that he would not notice at all, nor the village curate's wig which is nothing to him. But this feeble yet numerous school that calls itself realistic has, in my opinion, so little life and truth in its feelings and passions that it resembles the mathematician who was writing at his mother's death-bed: 'I lost my mother to-day at twenty-two and a half minutes past eight (mean time).' The passions are not so exact, and do not see so many things.

"In one of Tieck's comedies, a cat watching a nightingale says: 'This divine singer ought to be deliciously savory.' That is a cat that knows his business, and really has some feeling, and more art than the realistic school."

Doudan had that sensitiveness to unassuming merit that is only felt by warm, delicate, and generous souls. Such a soul is touched by the humble virtues, gentleness, modesty, patience, resignation, exquisite refinement of thought and feeling. An ignorant or a mean soul cannot feel these virtues, but must be startled into admiration by some remarkable feat of heroism, just as it must be dazzled by color or stunned by sound in order to feel pleasure in art or music.

Doudan feels all the merit, even though his wider range of thought makes him also feel the limitations of such a mind as that of Eugénie de Guérin, — a mind, clean, transparent, spiritual, not made for crowds but for green pastures and running brooks.

"She is provincial," he writes, "but she has a poetical soul. She possesses the magic wand which beautifies everything around her. Although she is superstitious, the natural elevation of her mind gives to her superstition a touching and amiable character. The little things of life become to her a subject

of meditation that transports her into the
most beautiful regions. On the contrary,
there are so many that set out with grand
ideas only to end in wretchedness; as witness the crowd of religious devotees. I am
surprised that you do not think her lot a
sufficiently unhappy one. She is poor, iso-
lated; she has lost all her people; she sees
slowly dying the brother who alone is left
to her. She is of those families of poor
country squires whose daughters, either from
poverty or pride, cannot marry their equals.
She is ill; nothing is sadder than her writing to her brother when she wants to read a
pious book: 'Is the book dear? I should
like to read it.' A great many cages con-
fine birds that were made for the loftiest
flights. . . . I hope you will have more
kindly sentiments for Miss Brontë, who is
not at all like Mdlle. de Guérin; never com-
plains, works unceasingly, ignoring discour-
agement and earning her fame by the sweat
of her brow, without for a single moment
losing sight of the small as well as the great
duties of the family. . . .

"I am sorry 'Cranford' does not please
M. Marc Vernet. It seems strange to me
that he is so insensible to all the detail of

feelings, scruples, and anxieties that are concealed in these simple and good souls, especially since he has studied these various
sentiments in order to regulate them in
others.   But—to express myself quite fully,
as I am accustomed to do in my letters — I
have always thought that theological habits
make us lose sight of the true foundations
of human nature.   A physician who had a
little box containing a remedy for all the
ills, would not trouble himself much about
clinics nor the study of physiology.   That is
why we see the profound and delicate meaning of human nature diminish in proportion
as religious doctrines are restricted to a
small number of dogmas, and we apply them
everywhere and to everybody with a certain
confident monotony.   The too habitual idea
of miracle makes us neglect and soon con-
temn all the shades of human nature."

No one has better expressed than Doudan
the existence of distinct national tastes in
literature, and the reason why that which
appeals to the warmest sympathies of one
nation shall fall dead and cold on the ears
of another.   Writing of Goethe's "Elective
Affinities," he says: "There must be great
merit in the style of Goethe's language, for

those of his ideas that do not relate directly
to morality are either dull or puerile. But
very likely I do not understand him. A
man who listened impassively to a sermon
that made his fellow-auditors shed torrents
of tears, said coldly, 'I am not of this par-
ish,' and perhaps he was right. Each
nation has its chords of sensibility that are
utterly incomprehensible to another. It
would not surprise you if, on returning to
France after a long absence, the Englishman or Pole who accompanied you were less
touched than you by the indefinable charm
you felt in these walls, woods, and fields.
Every nation recognizes this indefinable
charm in its writers. We have less of it
than other nations, and that is one reason of
our universality. For a long time we have
been charged with saying generalities to all
the world. We manufacture the household
furnishings and fashionable articles, but the
thousand nothings that touch the secret
fibres of a family or a province are wanting
in our literature. The ringlet of the woman
you have loved cannot touch everybody. I
am very insensible to the merits of the
'Elective Affinities,' but I am not stupid
enough to deny talent to Goethe. But why

did 'Werther' move all the world and all the parishes of his day?"

The following is Doudan's judgment of Longfellow. He has been calling Diderot a lion, and continues: "As for Longfellow, he is not that at all. He is a bird of the tropics, a little too blue and red, a little too sweet a singer. He has more elevation than force. He has great thoughts that come from the heart, as Vauvenargues says, but he lacks the energy of mind that gives them beak and claws."

Doudan is an admirer of Macaulay, and thinks that he has not the reputation in France to which he is entitled by virtue of the "extent of his knowledge, the delicate and profound culture of his mind, the brilliancy of his imagination, the abundance of just ideas and the good sense that rule his political sentiments;—the intimate knowledge of men and the singular mixture of impartiality and passion that is found scarcely anywhere but in him."

Doudan has for Sainte-Beuve the warm admiration of a critic who knows the range of culture, the coolness of judgment, and warmth of feeling required by true criticism. Writing at the time of Sainte-Beuve's death,

he says: "When Cousin died, it seemed to
me that there was now wanting to all the
noteworthy events of the world a passionate, eloquent spectator, inexhaustible in
original and unexpected commentaries. It
is the same with Sainte-Beuve. No book
worthy of attention will appear, but we shall
turn towards the judge who is gone. . . .
His was a species of criticism very rare in
our day, — at the same time wise and lively,
full of an enthusiasm that removes nothing
from sagacity. . . . In the criticism of great
writers, he united the labors of a Benedic-
tine monk with the penetrating imagination
of a nervous woman; the courage to say
everything while preserving all the shades
of justice; the taste for exactness and passion for truth of a Courbet with the sentiment of the ideal of Ingres himself. He
had a prodigious knowledge of all departments of literature, and at times the easy
flight of a bird over the surface of things.
. . . I find his 'Causeries du Lundi' very
much inferior to the 'Nouveaux Lundis.'
In the first he has not yet decided to tell
people the truth and all the truth. He is
still full of cajoleries towards Cousin, whom
he detested, and towards M. Villemain,

against whom he nursed a mute wrath. At that time he was a civilized cat with velvet paws. In the 'Nouveaux Lundis' he said, with a very few exceptions, all that he had in his heart, and, doubtless, from his little cottage at the foot of Mt. Parnassus he took pleasure in noting the effects of his judgments, regardless of the *amours-propres*, which are naturally unlimited."

In one of his later letters Doudan sums up the causes of his distaste for the popular literature of his time.

"My dear Friend, — I fear that we are growing a little old by the way in which we are disgusted with our era. I sometimes make an effort to conquer my own impressions, and to see whether the disgust I feel does not proceed from the fact that my habits of thought have grown too imperious with time to understand the habits of this new intelligence, if intelligence it be. But in looking well into the matter, I cannot fail to recognize that I am right in being irritated with this empty and declamatory tone; these fanfaronades of ideas that recoil before nothing; this contempt of distinction between good and evil; these impossible emotions that are feigned to be felt; these contradic-

tory passions supposed to exist in the same
creature; this pedantic, outrageous language;
these vivid colors and images to reproduce
such cold thoughts; the want of moderation,
harmony, good sense, and seemliness of all
kind which is spreading in literature, — all
these accusations are founded on irresistible
evidence; and if hanging were the penalty of
such guilt, many a writer ought to be making preparations for death.

"But perhaps in this devil's caldron where
the witches make their frightful broth, there
is one straw which is not solely noxious. A
single point of view to be caught sight of in
this labyrinth, merits arresting the eye. All
the literatures that we admire are simple and
harmonious; all the features are distinct,
clear, and brilliant. But such literatures are
romantic in this sense that they isolate, in an
ideal and luminous region, the object which
they wish to depict, and that in this excessive contemplation they forget all the relations that the object sustains to what remains
outside of the frame. To-day, on the contrary, we seem possessed with the rage of
demonstrating that everything acts upon
everything else, that a continuous chain
unites all creatures to all things. Not a

line is written that does not try to include
the history of the world. Have you ever
seen the ocean in a fury? Each wave on
this agitated surface takes its form of movement from all the waves that surround it
from the shores of Brittany to the glaciers
of the pole. It is an effort to express this
rebound of every part upon the whole, which
at present makes the grimaces of literature.
Hence these strained forms in which each
word plays a rôle; hence all these prismatic
colors lavished at every turn, this claim of
each sentence to be an echo of all the noises
in the world."

The extracts given above are a sufficiently
clear demonstration of the trend of Doudan's
thought and the style of his criticism.
Essentially, he is neither a teacher nor a
preacher; he is the scholar and the gentleman, the man of taste and judgment, the
friend of learning and of learners; and as
such, he stands for morality and good taste,
and will admit of no separation between
them. He believes in the humanizing and
elevating influence of the ideal; but by the
ideal he does not mean romantic extravagance, such as led Don Quixote to battle
with windmills. He has no sympathy what-

ever with those characters in purely romantic novels whom he calls the "descendants of chimeras, begotten like tiny insects between the leaves of books, moving by the agency of mechanical springs instead of blood and nerves." By the ideal he means those lovable and admirable transformations of a fine, clean imagination that gilds its tasks and its surroundings with generous thoughts of them, that prefers beauty to ugliness, and dwells by preference on whatsoever things are pure, true, just, lovely, and of good report.

VI.

GUSTAVE PLANCHE.

IT is easy enough to follow a beaten track through a wilderness. It is the man who first breaks it, whose face is scratched, whose hands are torn in its thickets, and whose arm knows the resisting strength of its interlaced branches, — it is he who knows all the weariness and difficulty of the accomplished task, and it is to him that our gratitude is due when we walk with easy and unembarrassed strides where he fought his way inch by inch.

Wherever you find the pioneer, and no matter what the character of his work, you will find the same qualities. He is the pioneer by the very nature of that adventurous, independent, fearless spirit in him. He is a man for whom there are no lions in the way, — the man whom you cannot make poorer though you strip him to the skin, for he carries his wealth in himself and not in his purse. His is the eye that sees, the ear that hears, and the hand whose cunning never fails him. His is the brain that feeds his heart with generous, courageous thoughts which are light and warmth to him in the darkness and cold of solitude and hardship.

The man, Gustave Planche, to whom our attention turns at present was of this pioneer type. He was born at Paris on the 16th of February, 1808, and he died in one of the charitable hospitals of his native city on the 18th of September, 1857. His death was the result of an abscess on his foot.

Émile Montégut has chosen Planche for one of the subjects of his volume entitled "Literary Sketches," and closes his article on this eminent critic with the following eulogy:—

"Even though coming generations, more and more distracted and busy, should find no time to read his works, he will not be forgotten. His name will not perish. In future he makes part of contemporaneous history, and that history cannot be written without taking his influence into account, and narrating the vigorous reaction that he opposed to the excesses of the romantic school. He struggled much, suffered much to affirm his independence and make known the rights of his liberty, and his efforts were not in vain. We are gathering the fruits of his labors to-day, for he made a precious conquest for us. He completely emancipated criticism; he freed it from servitude; he withdrew it from the patronage of literary patricians. To speak the truth when he did to his misfortune, — to have that boldness, was an act of moral courage which, like all legitimate resistance, was treated at first as rebellion and revolt. At that time poets and artists were about to transform the republic of letters into an exclusive and despotic oligarchy. A new theory of divine rights was invented for the poet. The abuses that characterize all unlimited aristocracies were already manifest. The right of remonstrance or petition was regarded as insolence. Freedom of opinion was considered revolt, and the critic likened to the pamphleteer or libeller.

"Gustave Planche rose alone in the face of this aggressive and violent tyranny, and organized a vigorous democratic resistance. More than once he felt his strength give way, but he never grew discouraged, and

counted on right and time for the triumph
of his cause.

"To tell the truth is no longer so dangerous a thing as it was, and the poet or artist
who should now think himself exempt from
the common law, would quickly find his position an absurd one. He might assemble
his clouds and hurl his poetic thunderbolts,
but it would be all in vain. The ridiculous
Jupiter would soon fall before a storm of
jeers and hisses. To-day we can frankly
say what we think without too great fear of
haughty insolence or insidious underhand
dealing. But in the quiet and peaceful exercise of critical rights exempt from fears
and persecutions, let us not forget that we
owe the free exercise of these rights to Gustave Planche."

In Gustave Planche we have the pure
critic, the man born to his calling, and early
recognizing that this calling alone has any
real claim upon his constant attention. It
is a common experience that fathers are disposed to ignore the aptitudes and self-chosen
occupations of their children in favor either
of their own calling or one which seems to
them to promise better worldly success.

Gustave Planche's father was a wealthy

Parisian druggist, who had acquired not only riches but some celebrity in his calling. He was one of the founders and contributors of the "Journal of Pharmacy." He had set his heart on his son's succeeding him in his work, and for this purpose sent him to a school of pharmacy; but instead of attending school, our young hero with the artist eye, and brain on fire with literary ambition, was visiting the National Museum, passionately studying antiques and the masterpieces of art, reading enormously, and laying the foundation of that erudition and austere taste which were to make him the most formidable critic of his time. Four years of such fruitful but secret study passed, and the father, impatient at his son's progress, began to make inquiries as to whether or not he was ready to receive his diploma. When he learned of the manner in which his son had been employing his time, his rage and disappointment knew no bounds. A terrible scene followed, and the boy, driven from home with his father's curse on his head, entered upon that long, painful struggle and isolation which ended only with his death. Even when fame came to him and justified the course he had taken in following his instincts, the father never forgave him nor consented to see him, though the son wrote him many touching letters full of contrition and entreaties for pardon.

To the pain of these broken home-ties, which he felt with the keen anguish that belongs to a sensitive, loving heart, were added the humiliations and pains of grinding poverty. He had gone out penniless from the elegances of his father's house. He lived in a wretched garret. For a long time he munched his scrap of bread and cheese, and drank his beer at a miserable tavern, where the honesty of the patrons was startlingly questioned by the fact that the pewter spoons, knives, forks, and brass goblets were chained to the table.

His trousers were frayed, his coat greasy, his boots worn into holes, and his old, soft felt hat torn at the creases; but he wore his old clothes, if not with royal dignity, at least with the fine indifference of a powerful mind wholly absorbed in the things that belong to itself and not to its "house of clay." He had not imposed an easy task on himself. He had come to tell the truth to a world that does not want to hear the truth unless it appears in a seductive form, and he had no

such forms to give it. As a natural consequence, he made many enemies; and as they
could not attack his brain, they jeered at his
body. They made his poverty a crime in
him. They laughed at his huge belly; they
professed disgust for his dirty shirt, his
boot-heels worn off at one side, his ink-
spotted hands; but with a drop of that ink
and a stroke of his pen he was master of
them all.

Eugène de Mirecourt, who sometimes tells
the truth by accident or when it happens to
be more piquant than scandal, is responsible
for the following anecdotes, which serve, at
any rate, to show the popular ideas of Planche
during his lifetime.

"He concealed his address from all his
acquaintances, less from shame than from
love of isolation. If he were forced to accept an arm on returning home in the evening, he always bade his guide adieu before
coming to the street where he lived. If he
saw anybody following him, he turned and
took an opposite direction. A facetious
artist once amused himself by keeping him
walking the streets until three o'clock in the
morning. Planche walked on heroically,
and it was the indiscreet pursuer who wea-

ried first, and Gustave was able to go home
without being seen. For a long time it was
thought that he slept in the open air on the
pavements of the public streets, and he himself took pleasure in giving credit to this
report.

" 'Where are you lodging?' some one
asked him.

" 'I don't lodge,' he replied, 'I perch.'

" 'And where?'

" 'Champs-Élysées, third tree to the right.'

"When he changed lodgings, all his wardrobe could be carried in his hat, — a fact that
enabled him to dispense with hack-drivers,
who are great revealers of addresses. One
of the porters at a hotel was greatly surprised
to see Planche take possession of his room
with three false collars for all his linen.

" 'But, sir, where are your shirts?' asked
the porter, naïvely.

" 'Do me the favor,' replied Planche, 'of
explaining to me why you put on shirts.
Isn't it to show your collars? Very well,
there are three collars and all of them perfectly clean.' "

Gustave Planche had the openness and
sincerity of the man who touches realities
every hour of his life. "All who knew him

intimately," says Montégut, "loved and es-
teemed him.   His faults were those that
harm nobody, and his qualities were such as
interest every one.   Certain sides of his
character were singularly elevated, and made
him worthy the respect due to his freedom
and candor.   His enemies might revenge
themselves for his contempt of them by puerile jokes on the exterior accidents of his
toilet, but in the presence of his character
every well-educated man took off his hat.
. . . Unlike men whom we do not learn to
know but after many years' acquaintance, he
could be wholly understood at the end of an
hour's conversation.   There were no obscure
corners in this character.   He allowed himself to be seen at once, like a man who has
nothing to conceal."

He was capable of ardent attachments, and
perhaps the warmest friendship of his life
was that which he felt for George Sand.
He was only four years her senior.   He wit-
nessed the literary début of this remarkable
woman, and at once recognized the power of
her genius.   He aided her with his fine critical judgment and advice; he defended her
with his pen, and he fought a duel for her.
It is to be wished tnat the gratitude she

owed him could have expressed itself during his lifetime, rather than in the tardy
acknowledgment of his merits in her auto-
biography.

"I owe," she says, "particular gratitude
as an artist to M. Gustave Planche, a mind
purely critical but of great elevation. He
was very useful to me, not only because his
frank jeers forced me to give some attention
to my language, which I was writing with too
much negligence, but because his conversation, little varied, but very substantial and
of remarkable clearness, taught me a great
number of things. After a few months of
friendly intercourse which were very agreeable and very interesting to me, I ceased to
see him, for reasons that ought not to create
any prejudice against his character, which,
for my part, I have never had any reason but
to praise.

"But an intimacy with him was seriously
embarrassing to me. It brought me into
collision with other friends. All those
whom Planche had offended by his writings
or his speech considered it a crime in me to
admit him to my house in their presence,
and I was threatened with complete isolation
by the abandonment of my oldest friends,

who, they said, ought not to be sacrificed
to a new-comer. I hesitated a good deal.
Planche was unhappy by nature, and he
seemed to have an attachment and devotion
for me quite unusual in him. I should have
considered it cowardly to dismiss him in
view of the literary hatreds his eulogies had
drawn down upon me, but I felt that association with him was really hurtful to me in-
wardly. His melancholy humor, his theory
of universal disgust, his aversion for the indulgent spirit in things easy and agreeable
in art, and the analytical tension it was necessary to keep up when conversing with him,
threw me, in my turn, into a sort of spleen, to
which I was but too much disposed when I
first knew him. I saw in him an eminent
intelligence which generously exerted itself
to share its conquests with me, but which
had amassed them at the expense of its happiness, and I was still at that age when I had
more need of happiness than of knowledge."

And Planche, with his great, hungry heart
and its need of happiness, repulsed from his
home, now repulsed by his friend, hated by
the world at large for his candor, his quick,
penetrating eye that pierced all surfaces and
went straight to the heart beneath them, —

what of him? He had ceased to be useful to
her, ceased to be amusing, — that is all, and
when he calls again he shall find the door
shut in his face. In a volume entitled
" Literary Portraits," Planche has given us a
touching article on " Literary Friendships,"
which this experience with George Sand
doubtless inspired; but it is written without
any insidious allusion or any ill-natured bitterness. Under the soiled shirt and thread-
bare waistcoat there beat the heart of a
gentleman, and Planche continued to use
his pen loyally for the woman who had shut
her door on him. And yet it was the sharp-
est of pens, — a pen that could drop gall and
wormwood when it chose, — a pen that earned
for its writer the name of " Cruel Gustave."

Balzac, who had winced under its strokes,
revenged himself by depicting Planche as
Claude Vignon in his novel " Beatrix."
George Sand, in the same novel, is depicted
under the name of Félicité des Touches,
" that amphibious being who is neither man
nor woman, who smokes like an hussar,
writes like a journalist, and at this moment
lodges with her the most venomous of all
writers."

Even in the most extravagant caricature,

some recognizable features must be preserved, or the caricaturist misses his aim,
which is, first of all, instantaneous recognition.   Therefore, even in Balzac's spiteful
caricature, we may find some interesting exterior traits of our "cruel Gustave," the
"most venomous writer of his time," whose
cruelty is, after all, the greatest kindness,
being like that of the surgeon who removes
a gangrened limb to save a life.   Happy the
age that can boast such a literary surgeon !

Claude Vignon, as Balzac chooses to call
Gustave Planche, is a "proud and scornful
writer, who, while producing nothing but
criticism, has been able to give to the public and to literature the idea of a certain
superiority. . . . This young man, bald at
thirty-seven, has an immense forehead, broad
and high, and seemingly shadowed by clouds.
His resolute, discreet mouth expresses cold
irony.   Claude Vignon is imposing in spite
of the precocious degradation of a face once
magnificent, now grown livid.   Between the
ages of eighteen and twenty-five, he has almost resembled the divine Raphael; but his
nose, that feature of the human face that
changes most, has sharpened, while, his
physiognomy having sunk, so to speak, under

mysterious depressions, the contours have
filled up with bad color. Leaden hues pre-
dominate in this complexion. . . . The eyes,
light blue, once brilliant, have been veiled
by unknown sorrows, or dulled by gloomy
dejection. Intemperance has left its trace
in the dark circles under his eyes. The
chin of incomparable distinction has grossly
doubled. His voice, never sonorous, has
weakened; without being either extinguished
or hoarsened, it is between extinction and
hoarseness. The impassibility of this fine
head, the fixity of this glance, conceal irresolution and weakness which are betrayed in
the sarcastic and intelligent smile. This
weakness is one of action, not of thought.
There are traces of an encyclopedic comprehension in this forehead and in the expression of this face, which is at once childlike
and haughty. There is a single detail which
can explain the eccentricities of his character. The man is very tall, slightly stooped
already, like those who carry a world of
ideas. These tall, large bodies are never
remarkable for continued energy or creative
activity. Charlemagne, Narses, Belisarius,
and Constantine are very uncommon exceptions to this rule. Claude Vignon certainly

offers mysteries to be divined. He is very
simple and very ingenious. Although he
easily falls into excesses, his thought remains unalterable. This intelligence which
can criticise the arts, science, literature,
politics, is unskilful at controlling the exigencies of exterior life. Claude contem-
plates himself in the extent of his intellectual
kingdom, and abandons his body with the indifference of Diogenes. Satisfied with understanding and penetrating everything, he
despises material things. But attacked by
doubt, as soon as it is a question of creating,
he sees obstacles without being ravished by
beauties, and in the discussion of means his
hands are idle and nothing is done. He is
the intellectual Turk whom meditation has
put to sleep. Criticism is his opium, and
his harem of books disgusts him with work.
Indifferent to the least as to the greatest
things, he is obliged by the very weight of
his brain to fall into excesses in order to be
released for some moments from the power
of his omnipotent analysis."

Beneath all this jumble of contradictory
words and ideas, this semblance of explanation without explaining, it is not difficult to
disentangle the real man, nor to see that the

caricaturist is conscious that he has a man to
deal with and not a charlatan, — a man of
learning and searching analytical power, and
not a mere journalist. In his description of
this man, Balzac cannot wholly lay aside the
favorite epithets of the romantic school, —
"divine," "magnificent," "imposing," "mysterious," "omnipotent;" and extravagant as
they are, even in this connection, perhaps
Balzac never made a less improper use of
them, for if human nature can afford a
"magnificent, divine, and imposing" spectacle, it is most assuredly that of a strong
and fine intelligence setting itself the task
of rescuing truth and stemming the tide of
error at the expense of all its happiness and
all its worldly advancement. Surely we can
pardon to such a man, in the heat of the
struggle, the disorder of his dress and the
roughness of his hands. We cannot lose his
work for the sake of a dress-coat and a pair
of kid gloves. This man gave all he had, —
his time, his youth, the vigor of his man-
hood. There is certainly an autobiographical touch in the following paragraph taken
from one of his articles, that may help us to
draw a little nearer this original, self-iso-
lated mind that has so many mysteries for

Balzac: "I have known some singular characters of an austere and permanent peace, who, while scarcely on the threshold of their years, disdaining the youth that flutter around them, were eager to grow old before their time. They were ambitious to feel under their yellow tresses the thoughts that ordinarily mature only under bald and wrinkled foreheads. These characters take sensual pleasure by its pitiless and terrible side. They kill their senses to disengage their souls. They lacerate the body to open to the intelligence larger horizons and more distant perspectives. Beyond the pleasures they prescribe for themselves and enjoy to the full, they perceive the serene atmosphere of thought."

It was in this atmosphere alone that Gustave Planche could breathe fully and freely. He carried it about with him, and it made him independent of material surroundings. He realized almost literally the poet's boasted satisfaction with "a hollow tree, a crust of bread, and liberty." Poverty pinched him the sorest where it laid restrictions upon his mental development. He knew a hunger fiercer than that which attacks the body, the hunger of the mind. To him completion of life meant complete mental development.

"Count the men," he writes in an article on Sainte-Beuve, "whose life is complete, — I do not say in the most absolute sense, — but the men who, without losing any of their faculties, choose one of them to carry it to the ultimate limits of its development; count the men who know how to love to renunciation, who know how to understand and sound truth without any other care than for truth herself, without any underlying thought of profit or renown, who know how to will and how to pursue the accomplishment of their will to the contempt of danger, who give to their resolution the proportions of an heroic struggle, — count them and you will understand that human life, severely interrogated, is, for the most part, but a succession of abortive feelings, ideas and resolutions. Transient emotions, confused perceptions, ephemeral desires, — that is the ordinary tissue of our days. The passions which bring forth devotions, the ideas which are transformed into glorious works and fertile discoveries, the desires which in persistence become resolves and inspire heroic actions, are the possessions of a few rare souls. The

rest make a feint at living, and do not live
at all.

"What rôle does sensual pleasure play in
this impoverishment of our faculties? Nothing is easier to determine. The pursuit of
pleasure every hour and on every occasion
leaves no time for the development of feeling, intellect, or will. Egotism and idleness
soon destroy all conceptions of right and
duty. Accustomed to regard pleasure as the
supreme and constant aim of life, we listen
with a smile to the history of actions that
are inspired by generous sacrifice. We feel
contempt and pity for those intellects that,
amorous of truth, consume their nights in
laborious watches in order to enlarge the
domains of science. We treat as madmen
those who stake their life to take their rank
among the heroes. Satisfied with the pleasures of the senses, we despise those who rise
above them, and when we realize the depth
of the abyss into which we have fallen, and
make a desperate effort to remount to morality, when we try again to grasp love, intellect, will, we too often fail in the tardy
effort. We have grown enervated in the long
sleep of the nobler faculties, for we have
sought the intoxication of the senses only

to obtain sleep for the soul, and the struggle instead of re-establishing our strength quickly exhausts us and we return to darkness and nullity.   Our eyes can no longer endure the light, and life that is truly worthy of the name has become a punishment for us."

The history of effort, of persistent will, of difficulty met and overcome, touched Planche more nearly than anything else, because it spoke to his own experience: "History is full of salutary lessons to me," he says. "We are comforted and calmed by the spectacle of sorrows that have preceded ours. And so I never read without being deeply touched one of the wisest books of England, — Samuel Johnson's 'Lives of the Poets.' I very readily pardon the author's grave pedantry, the affected emphasis of his doctrines, and the Puritanism of his taste in favor of the anecdotes and traditions that he has gathered with such religious labor.   Milton a schoolmaster! Savage writing in the street or in a smoky tavern on a borrowed piece of paper the disordered scraps of his poems! Do you know many novels so rich in touching emotions?"

In 1840 a small fortune reverted to Planche,

and released him for a time from the ceaseless grind to which he had been subjected.
He had nearly burnt his eyes out with study.
He was young, and could still profit by the
stimulus of fresh environments. He was in
sore need of rest, and he took it. Poverty
and struggle had nothing new to teach him,
and no experiences so bitter that he could
not endure them or could fear meeting them
again. There was one experience he had
not tasted, — that of spending his francs as
if they were grains of sand, and he the
owner of Sahara's desert. That experience
was possible to him, — for a limited period,
at any rate. He set out for Italy, and for
five years nothing was heard of him at Paris.

In Italy he gave himself up to the study
of art and music, to which he had always
been as much devoted as to literature. The
result of his labors was a volume entitled
"Études sur les Arts." Raphael, Rubens,
Rembrandt, Mozart, Beethoven, and Meyer-
beer are the principal themes of this volume, which abounds in acute judgments on
music and painting. "Many among us,"
writes Montégut, "who would not like to
confess it, owe to Planche our knowledge of
the difference between a good painting and

a seductive painting, — between an original school and an imitative school, and the fact that French art is not above Italian art, nor the Spanish superior to the Flemish school."

We have a number of apocryphal stories about Planche's extravagances in Italy, but one thing is certain. At the expiration of five years he was back in Paris with no increase in his wardrobe and nothing in his pocket. The grind recommenced. His criticisms on music and art brought him fame if not wealth, and won him the esteem of the Emperor, Napoleon III., who offered him the direction of the Academy of Fine Arts. He refused the directorship to escape any temptations that might assail his independence as a critic. This independence was the birthright that no humiliation, no suffering, no bribe could tempt him to sell. He had, to use his own language, one of those " inflexible minds which pursue truth under all its forms, which will not pardon in favor of popularity if it be unjust, nor of talent if it be a liar, nor of science if it lead astray; which in the appreciation of a work put the idea above the man, and never consult anything but their conscience in pronouncing a judgment."

In his particular interest in a man's work independent of the man himself, Planche differs notably from Scherer, to whom the man was always more interesting than his productions. Scherer values the tree more highly than its fruit. To Planche, on the contrary, the tree exists for the sake of its fruit, and it is the quality of the latter that absorbs his attention. In his critiques he merely sketches the biographical and anecdotical part, and hurries on to a discussion of the author's works. To this discussion he not only brings what Balzac styles an "encyclopedic comprehension," but a rare sense of his duty as a critic, which is, according to his conception, to cultivate the public taste and act indirectly upon the mass of creative minds. He wishes to substitute, in public taste, the enjoyment of the beautiful for the tawdry, reality for affectation. "Grandeur in simplicity, chastity in grace, ideality in harmony,— such," he says, "are the constant elements of beauty." He feels that the "contempt of sincere, pure, and disinterested passion leads inevitably to the contempt of thought itself and all the works of thought; that pleasure, taking the place of love, diminishes the sympathies for poetry, paint-

ing, sculpture, and that, in its turn, contempt
for art impels the multitude to seek brutal
pleasures."

With all his austerity, there is nothing of
the prude in him. He believes that truth
has no side that may not become a glorious
theme for the imagination, but he believes
in modesty of expression for freedom of
thought. He would have a writer say all
that he wishes to say, without restriction,
without cowardice, but he would have him
find grave, chaste words for his boldest
thoughts. Ever behind the saying, he
wishes to see purity, not averting her eyes
from vice, but pointing to it for its amelio-
ration, in clear, white daylight, and not in
the factitious light of a morbid imagination
that lends to it a false brilliancy and fatally
seductive charms.

The severest of Planche's criticisms are
now accepted by all men of the finest taste
and judgment. But at the time they were
written, they excited the greatest indignation. We have already learned from
Montégut something of the servile, fulsome,
and shallow character of the criticism of
Planche's day; but we shall get a better in-
sight into its character by Planche's own

arraignment of it, and we shall learn, too,
something of Planche's critical ideal.

"Where will you find frank and loyal criticism to-day?   Count on your fingers those
who make themselves hoarse in shouting
what they truly think.   Count them, and tell
me if ever language has been more scanda-
lously prostituted?   There is a kind of criticism which is very much in vogue at present.
Its business is not to study long in order to
have a just opinion; to pass its nights in
reflection in order to discern the true meaning of a book and to search afterwards the
clearest and purest form for its thought.   It
pities such childishness.   What it wants is
not a just opinion, but an opinion to put on
sale.   It keeps a shop in a public place, —
mud for those who despise it, incense for
those who pay.   The loungers know nothing
about literature, and are very glad to have a
ready-made opinion. . . . Yes; nowadays
language is a commodity, like the youth and
beauty of starving women. . . . Another
plague of criticism — a plague which, though
it has nothing disgraceful in it, is not, however, without its seriousness — is indifference. . . . Peaceful in the midst of his
knowledge, the indifferent critic compares

the present and the past without coming to
any decision.   He sees in the literary gymnasium only a distraction for his leisure.
He amuses himself with the poetical names
of all ages, and looks upon the glories that
come and go without being saddened or inspired.   He permits himself the spectacle of
the production, but he does not allow himself
to sympathize with the author.   He fears to
trouble the serenity of his thought. . . .
One thing absorbs him beyond anything
else, and that is the preservation of his
peace of mind.   Whenever he takes up his
pen he considers his own comfort and not
the truth.   He never asks himself: Is it
useless to blame, is it wise to approve what
is before me?   Would it not be just to encourage this voice which has not yet found a
hearing, to encircle with glory this young
brow?   Are n't there some profound thoughts
in this poem, unperceived as yet by the vulgar eye, — thoughts that have found no applause, and need to be interpreted in order
to be valued?   No; instead of that, without
troubling himself in the least about the value
of the book, he says to himself: Whom shall
I meet to-night?   The family and the friends
of the author.   Let us treat him with con-

sideration, for we must quarrel with nobody.

"The indifferent critic knows that to speak
frankly is to condemn himself to live alone.
He would not like to meet in a salon a face
embarrassed at his approach; and therefore
he will be careful to give an inoffensive
expression to his thought. Consequently,
what power there is in his remarks! . . .
He sits down to his task without ardor or
indignation; he spares the reader neither
exposition nor episodes. He never hazards
thinking for himself. He limits himself to
the rôle of a reporter. But he fills his rôle
completely and without reserve. . . . Only,
don't ask him whether he approves or con-
demns. He has no answer for such questions.
Prudence requires him to be silent. . . .

"There is another kind of criticism, severe, vigilant, impartial, that recognizes no
other law than its own conscience, no other
aim than truth. . . . Of what use is sincere, alert, disinterested criticism? Can it
aid the progress of literature? Can it influence the author and the public? Doubtless
the creative imagination will voluntarily abstain from consulting criticism. . . . It will
be satisfied with itself, and having finished its

work will resolutely say, 'I am right.' Let
it do so. I do not blame such a course.
But after this self-satisfaction has lost its
edge, the author needs fame. After the testimony of his consciousness, he wishes popularity. Here the critic rightfully comes to
his aid. Take the finest novel, 'Ivanhoe,'
the finest tragedy, 'Romeo and Juliet,'
and call the crowd. Do you think it will
yield itself naïvely to its admiration? Do
you think it will dare to be moved, and that
it will not blush for its tears? Yes, if you
mean the ignorant and vulgar crowd, — the
laboring and illiterate who have not time
to forget their nature; but, no, if you mean
the crowd that flutters in drawing-rooms
and the counting-houses, — the crowd depraved by morbid curiosity. For this half-
educated multitude that fill the boxes of your
theatres and concert-halls, there is needed a
vigilant authority to cry hourly to them in
the presence of the finest creations of the
human mind: 'Applaud without fear! You
will not be compromised by tears and applause. Emotion is your right. Be happy;
admire; you will not be obliged to retract
to-morrow an imprudent suffrage given to-
day. I am watching without relaxation in

the interests of your vanity. Like a faithful cup-bearer, I taste the wines that are served at your table. Drink and intoxicate yourselves. The joy is harmless, and the awakening without dishonor. For such service, independent criticism justly merits a little gratitude. . . . If patient reflection could not perceive and signalize any but superficial merits, if study and comparison could not surprise by analysis any but the beauties that are revealed to every one, criticism would no longer exist. It would have neither value nor individual force; it would be confounded with the conversation of drawing-rooms, the indecisive reveries of the promenade; it would write and cry in vain; opinion would remain deaf to its authority."

In Sainte-Beuve, Planche sees a critic whom he can heartily approve: "Sainte-Beuve tells the truth for the pleasure of telling it. He popularizes the names disdained by ignorance or frivolity. . . . He walks along his chosen road and acquires fame for himself in giving fame to others. When he meets a poet whose voice is scarcely heard, he applies himself unceasingly to enlarging its audience. He constructs a the-

atre with his own hands; he himself arranges
the acoustic tubes which are to magnify and
convey the sound to the most distant and
inattentive ears. Then, when the audience
is seated to listen, he watches the astonished
faces with a vigilant eye, to spy out inatten-
tion or want of understanding, and, like the
choir of the ancient tragedies, he moralizes
the crowd, and unfolds to them the mysteries
of the symbols at which they ignorantly
wonder. . . . He has lent a brotherly hand
to many a shipwrecked person who, on
touching shore, has forgotten the name of
his savior. He has covered many an obscure soldier with the imperial purple. . . .

"Before his time French criticism was
neither learned nor severe; it was scarcely
anything more than a vulgar enough sifting
of precepts and formulas whose meanings
were lost. To Sainte-Beuve belongs the
honor of putting poetry into criticism. It
was he who first made of the analysis of literary works something living and sparkling,
— capable of exciting interest by its own
merits irrespective of the work which served
as its point of departure. . . . Each of his
studies is a veritable voyage. He returns
to us from his adventurous journeys as from

17

a distant country. He shakes from his feet
the sand of unknown shores; he carries in
his hands the stems of unfamiliar plants
which he has gathered on his road. Nor
need we be surprised, if, like all travellers,
he is somewhat impregnated with the customs and the passions of the people among
whom he has been visiting, and in his turn
boasts of the temples of Bombay, Memphis,
and Athens, and confesses so many religions
that we might take him for an infidel. No,
this perpetual mobility is but constant good
faith. In each of his initiations Sainte-
Beuve never loses sight of Francis Bacon's
saying: 'The disciple must believe.' He
believes in Saint-Martin and Lamartine, in
Chateaubriand and Lamennais, in Diderot
and the Abbé Prévost; but for him, to believe is only a manner of understanding.
He believes in order to know; he studies
with the heart as women do, and like them
he yields himself in order to obtain. The
new faith which he accepts has nothing artificial or irresolute in it. By dint of contemplating his new friend, he is transformed
into his image; he begins to live his friend's
life; he evokes the shades of a society that
no longer exists; he awakens extinct pas-

sions; he reconstructs characters and resolutions that are impossible in our day; — and all that with such good grace, with such perfect naturalness, that we yield to the illusion with him. Each of the models that he poses before us, gains our affection by revealing some unexpected merits. It may be that more severe and less expansive intellects repudiate some of Sainte-Beuve's admirations. There are serious souls full of candor and sincerity that do not so easily yield to sympathy as he does; but he disarms reproach by the sincerity of his opinions. He is happy to admire as others are happy to understand."

Planche himself belongs to these "serious souls full of candor and sincerity." He says that truth in literary discussions is worth something more than elegant sentences, and that he would willingly give a dozen well-dressed, coquettish phrases for three just, reasonable words. " Let artisans become artists, rhymers poets, and we shall be the first to clap our hands. Until these marvels are realized, let us patiently resign ourselves to rare and sincere admirations. Let us not prostitute our eulogies to all rhymes drawn up in line; for our voice in degrading itself will lose the right to salute serious glories."

The idea of preparation for both literary and artistic work is one that often recurs in Planche. He is no believer in improvisations. He believes that the development of elevated sentiments requires a patient education; that before painting or modelling, the artist must first learn to think, must first sound the problems that excite intelligent curiosity; that before writing, the author must slowly and patiently accumulate and select with the severest care the thoughts that he offers to the public.

When he hears that Chateaubriand translated "Paradise Lost," and summed up the history of English literature in eighteen months, he says: "Unless the author, in the midst of his political life, has found means of reading and re-reading the historians, philosophers, and poets of Great Britain, which appears doubtful, it is evident that he was not prepared for the task he had undertaken. It is not in a few months alone that he could have made himself able — I shall not say to study, but simply to perceive, the innumerable questions with which the history of English literature is filled. I grant that

if he knew English he might have translated
'Paradise Lost' in eight months. But I
shall never admit that a year was sufficient
for him to read, compare, and judge all the
literary monuments from the time of the
Norman Conquest down to our day, — that
is to say, all the thoughts expressed by a
great nation in the space of seven hundred
and seventy years. The very announcement
of the problem is an affirmation that M.
Chateaubriand has not solved it. Had he
been laborious as Leibnitz, he could not have
accomplished, in the space of a year, a work
which embraces so many subjects, and of
which the very materials could not have been
collected by the most active and penetrating
intelligence in so short a time. . . . We do
not like trials of skill, and we do not think
that they profit anybody."

Planche accuses Eugène Sue of a superficial acquaintance with historical facts; tells
him that in his works farce, buffoonery, and
caricature are wedded to melodrama, and
form a medley that no serious critic can
treat as literature without forgetting his
duties and mission. He concludes his censure by warning him that it is to study and
to labor that renown legitimately belongs.

He criticises the French Academy severely
for opening its doors to Eugène Scribe, who,
he says, is incapable of a great work, and has
always treated good sense and grammar with
the most absolute contempt.   He wishes the
Academy to admit only those candidates who
are truly literary.   He wishes it to precede
and not to wait for popularity; to dominate
public opinion instead of servilely following
it.   In literature as in the army, he would
have honorary degrees won by the sweat of
the brow.

He explains Scribe's success by saying
that "The crowd likes to hail its old jokes
again and again.   It likes to applaud itself
for a clairvoyance that is no expense to its
attention.   It likes to proclaim itself intelligent and ingenious, and hails with gratitude the *bons mots* to which it has listened a
hundred times.   The more a thought seems
worn-out, the greater are its chances of success with the crowd.   M. Scribe owes the
best part of his success to his perfect knowledge of this fact. . . . He has taken for his
gospel this incomparable maxim: 'The rich
are right in being rich, and the poor are
wrong in being poor.'   Sifted down to their
fundamental expression, Scribe's comedies

have no other conclusion than this : Get rich,
no matter how, and the esteem of the world
will not fail you; but if you are fool enough
to get entangled in a sincere passion, you
will be the laughing-stock of honest folks, —
that is to say, the laughing-stock of people
who are well-born or have become rich."

No critic ever had a keener eye than
Planche for the detection of veneering. No
matter how high the polish, how skilful the
imitation of color and grain, he is too familiar with the solid wood to be deceived an
instant. When Chateaubriand's name was
still a name to conjure by, and his "Genius
of Christianity" could still find popularity
and applause, Planche wrote of it: "It is a
book written for idle women and for young
people whose life is spent in gaming, fenc-
ing, and horsemanship. For serious minds
that make reading something else than a
distraction, it is poor nutriment, a fruit
without savor, an exhausted plant, useless
dust. But this dust is brilliant and gilded;
it shines in the sun and pleases the eye.
The book means nothing, but the author
gives proof of rare skill. He never has philosophical clearness or Christian fervor, but
he has, everywhere and always, abundance

and poetic beauty. He is a speaker who
rarely thinks, but who talks very well, and
his audience, in listening to him, forget that
the imagery is egotistical and envelops but
a frail, scarcely apprehensible idea. . . .
Chateaubriand is a writer who sacrificed
being to appearing. His name will live
longer than his books. He is the author of
several hundred admirable pages, but he has
not written a single fine book."

But with all his strenuous insistence on
thought, Planche is by no means indifferent
to the merits of style, nor does he wish
erudition to take the place of poetry. He
demands the graces of art as well as the solidity of substance. He praises Guizot for
his industry and sagacity in collecting and
arranging facts; but he does not find in the
expression of his ideas, the least trace of
composition, and terms his " Essais sur
l'histoire de France," simply a mass of material, valuable to be sure, but wanting in
literary form.

In an article upon the state of dramatic
literature in France, Planche has given us
an admirable exposition of his theory of art
which will help us to understand the point
of view on which his criticism rests.

"M. Dumas," he writes, "has all serious artists against him. Music and architecture have evidently nothing to do with the question; and painting and sculpture, which, by the methods they employ, seem at first sight to be more rigorously allied than poetry to imitation of nature, have always, in the hands of eminent men, been an interpretation, and never a literal copy of the model. Take painting and sculpture in the most splendid epochs of their history, and you will never find them separated from interpretation, that is, from the ideal. Now, what is true of the plastic arts is no less true of poetry. If form and color, in their interpretation of the human model, are obliged, in order to render it intelligible, not to reproduce it slavishly, but to efface here and exaggerate there; language, in proposing to itself a similar task, ought not to be exempt from the conditions we are about to set forth. If marble and canvas, in imitating the model, cannot dispense with invention, neither has language the privilege of attaining to poetry by literal imitation. I know very well that the multitude persist in seeing in M. Dumas' servile reproduction of nature the ultimate dictum of human art.

But in the face of a gross error or an obstinate ignorance, we must not fear attacking
the opinion of the majority.   If nature, servilely copied, is the last word of human art,
then the works of Phidias and Raphael are
very much inferior to the figures of Curtius.
If the genius of the artist is directly propor-
tional to illusion, then colored wax, clothed
in serge, is very superior to the sculptured
figures on the frieze of the Parthenon, or to
the frescos of the Vatican.   To profess in
good faith that nature, servilely copied, is
the highest expression of art in painting,
sculpture, and poetry, is never to have studied, never to have caught a glimpse of the
laws of the imagination either in the domain
of consciousness or in the domain of works
that are proclaimed beautiful by the unani-
mous consent of all cultivated minds.   To
sustain the doctrine of realism in art, is to
misunderstand the very cause of the admiration won by the master-pieces of art and
literature.   It is to be blind to beauty; it
is a confession of incapacity in all questions of æsthetics.

"But even were nature the supreme aim of
human art, even if interpretation were to be
erased from the list of poetic duties, still M.

Dumas would be very far from right in his calculation, for he has reproduced in his works only the grosser part of nature. He has resolved on copying man as he is, and he copies only the physiological element in him. He wishes to depict passion restored to its primitive laws, and, to be frank, he has not even divined passion; he has not depicted sentiments, he has depicted appetites. He has adorned with the name of love, the purely physical attraction of one sex for the other, and has never put on the stage true, pure, poetic love. Always and everywhere, he has substituted the animal for the hero, heat of blood for exalted hope. Far from idealizing the reality which he has before him, he does not even represent complete reality. Had he portrayed without omission the model which he wished to copy, he would not have ranked among the poets, but at least the poets would have understood him, even if they did not accord him the honor of fraternal sympathy. Had he wholly accomplished the task which he assigned himself, he would not have given proof of poetic power, but in displaying to the multitude, not only the element that poetry disengages and idealizes, but also the

useless and importunate element that it
neglects but does not misunderstand, the
crowd, unconscious of the useless element,
would have been indebted to him for emotions of an elevated order.

"In confining the drama within physiological limits, he has condemned himself to
perpetual repetition of a scene which never
varies, and of which the only actors are, and
always will be, the strength that desires
and the weakness that cannot defend itself.
There were yesterday, and there will be to-
morrow, spectators and applause for this in-
variable scene; but in literary discussion,
such a fact is an objection that has no
weight. . . . Popularity — I do not say
fame — does not come to works slowly conceived, composed in long watches, written
without haste and meditated at leisure. It
caresses and applauds works conceived without reflection, composed without discern-
ment, written by the ream for money, and
the ignorant count the pages which they
cannot judge."

The vigorous critical war that Planche
waged, and in which he made so many enemies, while winning victories for sound criticism, was directed against Hugo, Balzac,

and their followers. In 1838, when Victor
Hugo was thirty-six years old, and the most
popular poet of his day, Planche wrote a
critique in which he complained that Hugo
is wholly absorbed in the musical and picturesque features of his verses to the exclusion of their sense and feeling. "Hugo says
all that he wishes to say, but I must add
that he has nothing to say. Wholly absorbed in the evolutions of his strophes,
occupied in disciplining them, in making
them march by twos and threes, and in
dividing them into columns, he has not time
to ask whether these gilded ranks that glitter in the sun are as ready for war as for
parade. Proud of their docility, he regards
them with a fond and joyous eye, and in this
childish pleasure forgets the most imperious
of all the laws that govern poetry. He sings
for the mere sake of singing. He vocalizes;
he lavishes high notes and low notes; he
runs an octave in a minute, and does not
understand the very essence of poetry. He
forgets to feel and to think. With him, this
forgetfulness is voluntary and is formulated
into a system. Astonished at the ductility
he has been able to give to his words, he
soon comes to believe that poetry can do

without ideas and feelings; and I am forced
to acknowledge that this singular belief has
become contagious. The collection of poems
known as 'Les Orientales' has, for a great
while, appeared to the disciples of M. Hugo
the greatest triumph that poetry can obtain.
Without misunderstanding the richness and
brilliancy of this collection, we believe that
true poetry plays no part in the 'Orientales;'
because that poetry which is addressed
neither to the heart nor to the intellect,
which excites no sympathy, awakens no meditation, does not merit the name of poetry;
it is only child's play. There is not a page
in the 'Orientales' that either moves or in-
structs; not a page that bears witness that
the author has felt or thought, — that he has
been one of a family, of a state, or that he is
capable of joy or sorrow, that he has wept in
isolation and abandonment, or that he knows
the happiness of loving intimacy. The
strophes glitter and unroll with marvellous
agility; but the pleasure from the reading is
sterile, and leaves no trace in the memory. In
admiring the versifier, we search for the poet.

"Had M. Hugo, taught by experience,
dissatisfied with being misunderstood, proposed to himself suppleness of the strophe

as a means, not an end, had he multiplied
poetical forms with the intention of giving
more grace and lightness to his thought, we
should be the first to congratulate him on
this resolution. But it is evident that, in
the 'Orientales,' the strophe is everything
and the thought nothing. The author man-
ufactures his innumerable moulds, and, when
they are finished, he pours the hot metal into
them for the sole pleasure of seeing it run.
What happens? The metal cools and becomes rigid; but the bronze, in becoming
solid, does not become a statue." . . .

After as severe an analysis of Hugo's
other poetical works, Planche continues with
a consideration of the poet's novels.

"Although the three novels which have
preceded 'Notre Dame de Paris' are very far
from having the same literary importance as
this last work, a serious study of them is indispensable to an understanding and an explanation of the successive changes which
M. Hugo's talent has undergone. I know
that these changes are rather apparent than
real, rather superficial than profound. Iden-
tity is concealed under diversity. It is easy
to retrace in 'Notre Dame' the exploits of
'Han d'Islande,' and to conclude 'Han d'Is-

lande' with 'Notre Dame de Paris.' However, it is not out of place to analyze the first
three attempts that signalized M. Hugo's
entrance into the domain of romance, for
this analysis is not less rich in instruction
than that of his lyrics.   If the author of
'Notre Dame de Paris' were to publish
'Han d'Islande' to-day, such a book would
certainly obtain no success, would not even
raise a disdainful opposition.   In fact, this
novel is but a melodrama of the third class,
and doubtless it would have been forgotten
long ago, had it not been for the curiosity
that attaches to the first stammerings of
a celebrated writer.   Han d'Islande and
Spiagudry are hideous monsters and inspire nothing but disgust. . . . At the most,
the book is worthy of taking a place by the
side of 'Bluebeard.'   Therefore, it would be
unjust to insist upon its nullity; but it is
worthy of notice that M. Hugo's predilection for monsters is for the first time signalized in 'Han d'Islande.'

"In 'Bug Jargal,' we find this predilection betrayed under a less hideous form, but
with a perseverance that indicates an arrested
system. . . . 'Le Dernier Jour d'un Condamné' unfortunately sums up the defects

and qualities of the lyrical collection. . . .
The subject seemed to promise a psychological study. . . . There was reason to hope
that little by little the author would forget
his love of noise and color; that he would
unlearn his devotion to words and return to
thought and emotion by patient study and
diligent analysis of the theme he had chosen.
. . . We hoped to witness the tortures of
conscience, and we had before us only the
tremblings of the flesh.

"In 'Notre Dame de Paris,' we find in
full maturity all the literary qualities that
exist but in germ in the three preceding
works. . . .

"Do the characters in this book belong to
the human family? We do not believe it.
Is M. Hugo's literary talent richer, more
varied in this than in his earlier novels?
Yes, assuredly. The style of 'Notre Dame'
is incontestably superior to that of 'Han
d'Islande,' 'Bug Jargal,' or of 'Dernier Jour
d'un Condamné;' but this style, I regret to
say, is enriched at the expense of thought.
. . . The writer has become more skilful,
but the poet has strayed farther and farther
from human truth, without which there is no
poetry possible. . . .

"It is the spectacular that dominates the book and makes its success. 'Notre Dame de Paris' has succeeded, and yet it is far from being a good book. The problem is not to dispute an accomplished fact, but to explain it. In our opinion, the puerility of the author's work has found a powerful assistant in the puerility of the public taste. In writing 'Notre Dame,' M. Hugo has consulted the instincts of his time, and has succeeded because he consulted them. It is very true that seven years ago, France loved the spectacular in the drama, and preferred the poetry that speaks to the eyes to that which speaks to the intellect. No doubt, it was a depraved taste, — a taste that enlightened men combated with all their power; but it was the taste of the majority, and the majority was to applaud 'Notre Dame.' To-day, public taste has changed. It asks of poetry something else than delight for the eyes; and therefore the poetical merit of 'Notre Dame' is questioned.

"But we must not allow the reaction to carry us too far. If 'Notre Dame' is not a fine book in the highest sense of the word, it is distinguished by brilliant qualities which must not be overlooked. It would be unjust to refuse to recognize that. To speak frankly, the stone and the timber are the chief, I ought to say, the only, actors in the work. But never have stone and timber been put on the scene with more splendor, with more magnificence. Never has language found resources more abundant and varied for their description. If stone and timber cannot fill the frame-work of a novel, that is no reason for denying M. Hugo's picturesque merit. In painting, as in poetry, in all the great schools from the Florentine to the Flemish, man plays the first rôle; for Raphael, Titian, and Rubens, stone and timber are only the secondary parts of the picture. Yes, doubtless, but it is justice to say that M. Hugo has painted this secondary part with the skill of an artist of the first order.

"The importance given to stone and timber inevitably encroaches upon, if not effaces the importance of the human being, and, in fact, man in 'Notre Dame' is but a point on the stone. He fills out the timber and serves to show it off. It is evident that the author could get on better with the cathedral and without the deacon and sexton, than he could with the deacon and sexton and with

out the cathedral.   Quasimodo and Claude
Frollo are very effective under the arches of
the church, on the gallery which unites the
two towers, and on the fretted work that
crowns them, and the author draws them to
complete the picture.   But don't ask him to
bring nearer to you these two points that he
has baptized with the name of man; for, in
doing so, he would diminish the picturesque
effect of his church.   The stone and timber
would then be restored to the rank to which
they belong, and the pleasure of the eyes,
the only one he has in view, would no longer
be exclusively sovereign.

"There, if I am not mistaken, is the real
merit and the real vice of 'Notre Dame.'   In
this work so singular, so monstrous, man
and stone are confounded, and no longer form
but one and the same body.   Man under
the pointed arch is no more than the moss on
the wall, or the lichen on the oak.   Under the
pen of M. Hugo, the stone is animated and
seems to obey all the human passions.   The
imagination, dazzled for a time, thinks that
it witnesses the enlargement of the domains
of thought, — invasion of matter by intelligent life.   But quickly disabused, it per-
ceives that matter has remained what it was,

and man has petrified. The sculptured sal-
amanders on the flank of the cathedral have
remained immobile, and the blood that flows
in the veins of man has frozen; breathing is
arrested; the eye sees no longer; the be-
numbed soul has forgotten how to think.
Doubtless, in order to produce this singular
illusion, in order to aggrandize, even for a
moment, the domain of intelligent life, great
skill is required. We are far from disputing M. Hugo's skill; but this illusion, however transitory, is fatal to poetry; it turns
the multitude from serious pleasures, from
the pleasures of intelligence, and accustoms
them to puerile relaxations."

The article concludes with an analysis of
Hugo's dramas, which Planche thinks the
feeblest part of his works, because "of all
literary forms the drama is that which most
imperiously demands a knowledge of men,
and we have reason to think that M. Hugo
has never studied them." Planche also accuses Hugo of ignorance of history, warns
him not to trust to his genius alone, because
no knowledge is possible without study, and
concludes by promising that if Hugo renounces his puerility, grows greater in re-
generating himself, that he, the critic,

will forget his defects and applaud his victory.

Bulwer was at the height of his transient glory when Planche was writing, and the keen eye that pierced Hugo's rhetorical trappings was not to be deceived by Bulwer's superficial glitter. In a critical review of "Ernest Maltravers," Planche pronounces the book a very common novel with very little philosophy and very little literature in it. "In this book, as in the majority of his preceding works, the author gives proof of great ingenuity and very little imagination. It is true that M. Bulwer did not pretend to write a novel, and that he attaches a very great importance to the numerous digressions that fill a third of the book: but these digressions, far from concerning the characters of the book, amount to nothing more than a continual complaint. M. Bulwer, whose celebrity might appear exaggerated, not only to backbiting England, volatile and frivolous France, but even, I fear, to sage Germany, — that nation of critics and thinkers, — M. Bulwer, whom the reviews of Great Britain proclaim the successor of Walter Scott, and the whole of whose works is not worth a single chapter in 'Ivanhoe,' speaks of literary

life as one might speak of the galleys, the
pillory, or of hell. According to him, as
soon as an author becomes celebrated, the
salons and journals slander him every day:
the walls of his house fall before the insult-
ing glance of hatred and envy; his private
life is open to the most injurious comments;
he cannot take a step, change his cravat or
his manner of wearing his hair, or of showing his waistcoat without having these most
innocent actions construed by the press as
the most guilty intentions. Fame is a Calvary, and the author is crucified. In fact,
if M. Bulwer were not by profession a ro-
mancer, accustomed to confound invention
and reality, we should be filled with compas-
sion for the tortures of life on the other side
of the channel. But it is very probable that
fame in London, like fame in Paris, is a very
mild cross to bear. At London, as at Paris,
pride is condemned to cruel tortures, and
that is doubtless what M. Bulwer calls the
poetic Calvary. At present, the exaggerated
flatteries of the press have everywhere so
monstrously developed the pride of men who
strive for fame in publishing their thoughts,
that a eulogy accompanied with restrictions
very easily passes for calumny. To criti-

cise a barbarism is calumny; to censure the
vulgarity of incidents, — a calumny! The
critic has but one way of showing his loyalty
and probity, or, in a word, of meriting the
esteem and sympathy of the author, and that
is by boldly assigning to each of his works a
rank between Homer and Dante, Shakespeare and Goethe. And still, it would be
necessary to sound him prudently before
commencing any parallel, for poetic sensibility is at such a stage of delicacy at present, that it would be very easy to wound it
by a maladroit comparison. To attribute
something of Homer to him who prefers
Milton, or of Shakespeare to him who prefers Sophocles, is to be wanting in respect,
in comprehension, very likely it is to calum-
niate him.

"The style of 'Ernest Maltravers' is easy,
abundant, and at times even distinguished
by a certain elegance, but it almost constantly lacks precision and simplicity. The
best sentences are scarcely more than conversational sentences. Instead of choosing
for his thought a determined expression, to
the exclusion of synonyms which may present themselves, or near comparisons which
occur to the memory, the author sketches

several expressions and gives them to the
reader without caring to accept the responsibility of an irrevocable preference.   Such
a procedure indicates in the writer a familiar
acquaintance with the vocabulary, but, to
speak frankly, it is the very negation of style.
It is a system which dazzles for a time, but
ends by making the reader impatient.

"I regret that M. Bulwer feels himself
obliged to sow the conversation of his characters with several French phrases that are
sometimes vulgar and not always correct.
Well educated people who accost each other
among us, do not say, 'Comment ça va?' and
if they said it, they would not write it.   Nobody in France addresses his interlocutor
with '*des* belles paroles.'   When a woman
goes out riding alone with a gentleman, she
does not say that she risks 'le cavalier seul,'
for this expression, used in calling a quad-
rille, would have no application in her
case.   Certainly, it would have been better
not to prefix to the different chapters of
'Ernest Maltravers,' epigraphs taken from
Æschylus, Euripides, and Simonides, and to
transcribe correctly the French and Italian
words pronounced by the characters.   Erudition is not necessary, but modesty is always in good taste."

Michelet, the historian, is another writer in whom Planche wants a more rigorous, more logical, and clearer method, a renunciation of fancy and ecstasy, for an adherence to the demonstration of truth, — fewer features that belong properly to romance, and more sobriety of treatment. "He is resolved on touching or exciting the reader at any price, and that emotion which is not born of the very expression of truth, which needs all the artifices of the imagination in order to take possession of the reader, ought to be severely banished from history. . . . He mistakes a figure of speech for an idea. . . . Little by little, he has become accustomed to the ecstasy of the mind dazzled by study, as the Orientals to the hallucinations produced by opium. This state, so contrary to the development and exercise of the historical sense, has become his normal condition. That is the reason that if I wished to characterize his 'History of the Revolution' in a sentence, I should compare it to the recital of the 'Passion' written by sister Emmerich; it is not a history, — it is a vision."

In an article entitled "La Poésie et la Critique en 1852," Planche proposes to question successively fiction, poetry, and litera-

ture, in order to know what they signify at
that date; and having exhausted this inquiry,
he proposes to compare the popular works in
each of these departments of literature with
the demands of public intelligence. The
conclusions he reaches are singularly appli-
cable to the state of literature to-day, and it
is almost impossible to realize that a lapse
of nearly half a century intervenes between
our date and that of his inquiry. But the
fact is that popular literary judgments are always of the same essential character. They
proceed from a childish taste, which is invariably pleased with what strikes the senses,
and a childish superstition, which invariably
sees the supernatural in what it cannot explain. An appeal to its senses, or to its
love of the marvellous, will always catch its
suffrage and insure popularity, because, as
Planche somewhere remarks, "exquisite and
cultivated natures will never be a majority."

Planche begins his inquiry by asking what
the novel is to-day; for he recognizes that
"novel-making has become an industry that
can compete in importance with that of Shef-
field, Birmingham, or Manchester. Formerly," he continues, "the novelist naïvely
proposed the analysis of passions and char-

acter.   In the movement of ordinary life, he
selected an action of a very simple character, often apparently insignificant, and
counted on the study of the human heart to
interest cultivated minds.   That was the
golden age of the novel. . . . The capital
merit of these little compositions is sobriety.
The author never thinks himself obliged to
talk when he has nothing to say.   As soon
as he has exhibited all the phases of his
thought, and exhausted the analysis of the
passions which he has chosen to depict, he
stops, sure of having accomplished his task.
He does not exhaust himself in piling up
sonorous words to fill the place of absent
ideas.   This merit, so commonplace that it
brings a smile to the lips of industrious
writers, is nevertheless the key to renown.
To endure, to mean something, is not merely
a question of offering thought of some value
under a precise form to the public; it is also
necessary to stop talking, when one has nothing more to say.   It is impossible to calcu-
late the blessings of silence.   The public
not only takes into account the sensible
words you have written, but also the empty
words you have not written.

"To-day, all is changed, if not in the

opinion, at least in the practice of the trade,
for I cannot give the name of art to the fab-
rication of the novels which have deluged
the journals during the last twenty years.
Empty and useless words are no longer regarded as foolishness; it is sobriety alone
that passes for silliness. To speak when
you have something to say? A fine merit,
truly! But to speak when you have nothing
to say — that is what reveals true genius!
The triumph of the trade is to build twenty
volumes — thirty if necessary — on a subject that our modest ancestors would have at-
tempted to treat in some hundreds of pages.

. . . .

"To substitute the trade for the art, it is
necessary to change the fundamental and
elementary conditions of the novel. And,
in fact, those who like, or pretend to like,
this form of literature to-day, do not hesitate
to change the aim, in quitting the beaten
road. It is no longer a question of the
analysis of passions, — vulgar task worthy of
the narrow minds which preceded us, — the
question, now, is to excite, to amuse, at all
hazards. Provided the reader turns the page
with curiosity, with fear, the most exacting
mind can demand nothing more. Probabil-

ity, simplicity, interest founded on the study of the heart, are relegated to the rank of banalities and confounded with old fashions. To recall these vulgar precepts is as effectual as preaching the wearing of paniers, patches on the face, or red heels. . . .

"To have in view an aim to be reached, to foresee and trace the route to be followed — is not that to distrust one's genius? Foresight is a leading-string. There is but one god for purely fertile imaginations, and his name is chance. What is the use of knowing what you are going to say? Men devoted to the trade of authorship, animated with a legitimate confidence in their powers and a confidence no less legitimate in the sympathy, and especially, in the idleness of the reader, ought to walk without anxiety towards an unknown goal, ought they not? Whatever this aim may be, they are sure of attaining it. They are going nowhere, and yet their deliberate gait seems to indicate a well-defined project. It is enough if the reader follow them. For those who find their dearest pleasure in idleness, such stories are really a means of deceiving *ennui*, if not of getting rid of it, and it is not this class of minds that I am addressing, for the

soundest arguments are impotent in the presence of sluggishness and idleness. But for
those who know the charm of study and meditation, such work is an insipid dish, — a
tasteless fruit that they reject with disgust.
As well bite into dust and ashes.

"The sceptics reply: Why censure what
amuses? Why judge, in the name of a literary theory, works that are conceived in contempt of all theories? Why waste your
words in air? This objection does not re-
duce me to silence. This rage for amusement which has taken possession of readers
leads straight to enervation of mind. In
substituting curiosity for sensibility, in demanding every day incidents true or false,
but new at any price, — the multitude unconsciously loses its most precious faculties;
it can no longer distinguish nobleness from
triviality, heat of blood from generosity of
feeling. Little by little, it grows incapable
of poetic emotion. Its soul becomes dull
and depraved like the palate of a man who
abuses the use of spices and liquors. The
most wholesome, most excellent food seems
without savor to him.

"Let them tell me in all manner of ways
that I am preaching in the desert, I persist

in believing that I am right in putting my
finger on this literary plague of the century
in order to probe the wound and to predict
its approaching ravages. After enervating
the intelligence of the multitude, this novel-
writing trade will end by destroying the last
vestiges of æsthetic sense. Sated with this
gross food, the multitude will soon lose the
idea of the beautiful and the ugly, as it loses,
in drunkenness, the idea of justice and injustice, unless a voice is raised to warn it
from the mud into which it is about to fall."

From the novel, Planche proceeds with a
consideration of the drama, upon which he
passes an equally severe judgment, reproach-
ing it for putting costumes and stage-fur-
nishings above characters philosophically
studied, and history properly speaking, —
and for preferring accuracy of rhyme to accuracy of thought.

"The thought of great writers is developed like the oak, from the centre to the
circumference; it takes its logical form in
expanding. The thought of second-rate
writers is developed in the manner of the
palm, from circumference to centre. It is
born of an assemblage of words, as the trunk
of the palm is increased by the buds that

grow on its circumference. . . . I esteem
very highly the musical feature of poetry. I
want the ear to be satisfied. But I will not
consent to put language on the same level
with the violin and the flute. Speak melo-
diously, — very well; but, before speaking,
have something to say. If you count on the
mere jingle of words to reveal a thought,
you expose your imagination to singular
miscalculations."

Planche continues his article by counsel-
ling the new generation to study the inner
world, to explore the depths of consciousness, in place of enumerating the colors of a
toga or a surcot, a tabard or a tunic, and to
listen to the beatings of the human heart, instead of putting the hand on the studs of an
armor. Poetry receives a reprimand similar
to that given to the drama, and the author
concludes by saying that literature is corrupted by materialism, and that spirituality
alone can give it back its youth and brilliancy. "In proportion as poetry attributes
a great importance to the exterior world, man
will be degraded. Let matter redescend to
the lower rank to which it belongs; let the
spirit remount to the rank which it never
ought to have quitted, and art, renewed, will

find again the authority it has lost. It is my
prayer. It is my hope. It is the prayer
and hope of all sensible men."

In addition to his "Études sur les arts,"
and "Portraits d'artistes," Planche's published works consist of volumes made up
from his contributions to the "Revue des
deux Mondes," and other French journals.
These volumes appear under the titles of
"Études littéraires," "Portraits littéraires,"
"Nouveaux Portraits," and "Etudes sur
l'École Française."

The extracts we have given are a sufficient
guarantee of the vigorous spirit that animates all he has written. His word was all
he had; but it was pure gold, and he refused
to debase it by any alloy, for the sake of
making a profitable and convenient currency
of it. When his publisher refused to accept
an article on account of the effect its candor might give, he would destroy the article, but he would neither alter its judgment
nor temper its severity. He took his work
too seriously to be a witty critic, in the sense
of criticism searching for subjects of raillery
to amuse the crowd; but he abounds in that
wit which proceeds from good sense and a
keen perception of incongruities. He made

no demands upon others that he did not
doubly exact from himself. He spoke from
a fulness of just and reasonable ideas. As
for his character, one thing is certain: a
spring of cool, pure, refreshing water issues
from no foul ooze; it comes from rock and
crystal, where foulness cannot lurk. Whatever offence the outside of the platter might
give to the Pharisaical world, the inside was
unstained and white.

There were depths of tenderness in him
never opened to the sunlight, for life was
unkind to him; but there were living, not
stagnant, waters in those depths, and they
preserved him from that aridity of soul and
fatal coldness which so often follow the too
exclusive culture of the mind at the expense
of the heart. The sharpness of his pen came
from no love of cruelty, but from passionate
love of beauty and truth, which he saw
neglected for tricked-out ugliness and var-
nished falseness. He had tasted the deep,
pure pleasures of the intellect, and he burned
with a generous ardor to share them with
others. He tore down, in order to build up
something better; he took away what was
worthless, to give what was precious. He
received hatred and insult, instead of grati-

tude and reward; but he was neither si-
lenced nor transformed into a cynic. He
was a brave, honest, resolute man, large-
brained and deep-hearted, to whose memory
posterity willingly pays the gratitude with-
held from him in life.

VII.

CONCLUSION.

THE men whose works we have been studying offer us interesting contrasts in temperament and character. Scherer and Planche are purely men of letters. In each, the critical faculty is especially strong, but there the likeness ends. Scherer had not yet begun his critical work at an age when Planche had nearly completed his. Scherer's mental development embraces a wider field of experiences, and gives him a certain breadth, poise, and moderation wanting in Planche. He praises more willingly than he censures; he does not, like Planche, seek a cause to defend or an abuse to attack. If they come in his way, he will fight manfully, and with all the skill of an experienced swordsman; but he does not like fighting. He likes best to enjoy the undisputed realms of art. Planche, on the contrary, prefers the skirmishing on the borderlands. He dreads an invasion; he jealously guards the fron-

tiers.   He fears nothing, and will face can-
non and muskets alone, if need be.   One is
the born soldier; the other, the man of
peace, and each is needed in his place.

Saint-Marc Girardin and Bersot are both
professional men.   Both are intrusted with
the education of the young; both bring to
this work ardor, interest, capacity.   But
here, too, the likeness ceases.   Girardin is a
realist, and Bersot an idealist in the best
sense of these terms.   Girardin is keenly
alive to the dangers that beset youth on the
side of the imagination, — the abuses of rev-
erie and the errors of judgment.   He wishes
to arouse to action and to destroy illusions.
Bersot, with his poetical temperament, which
is the source of his purest joys, is more alive
to the dangers that beset youth on the side
of sterile materialism.   He wishes to render
the soul invulnerable to harsh and coarse
realities.   He would give it wings to soar
above its trials.   Girardin would give it a
pair of good, stout legs to carry it through
them.   Both are right.   Each complements
the other.   There is poetic invulnerability,
and the invulnerability that belongs to rare
good sense; and the soul that is not capable
of the one may hope to possess the other.

Doudan belongs to quite another order of men. He is pre-eminently the connoisseur. He enjoys literature solely and simply for its own sake. He belongs to no school and has no system to defend. His judgments are purely the result of his taste. He utters them as an epicure would express his preference for certain meats and wines, and he attaches little more importance to them as regards others. But his taste is exquisite and his utterances have a value that belongs to such taste.

But however much these critics differ in temperament, character, and form of expression, there is a remarkable unanimity in their literary judgments. Their whole criticism is based upon identical principles; and if we disengage these principles from the particular subjects under discussion, we shall find that they may be briefly stated as follows:—

(1) Art cannot free itself from the obligation to be moral, because it has to do with the beautiful and the normal. The beautiful and the normal are moral, because they exist in obedience to the general law; and morality is obedience to law.

(2) Art in its highest manifestations

addresses the intelligence, not the senses; it is less concerned with manner than with matter. It satisfies thought and not prurient curiosity and idle wonder. Its aim is not to amuse, but to delight the mind by an appeal to its noblest faculties, — its sense of justice, order, harmony, beauty, and purity.

(3) Art reacts upon human life. What we admire, in a great measure, determines what we are; hence, the necessity of right admiration, and the importance of morality in art.

(4) The soul finds its healthiest activity in mild enthusiasm, in elevated repose; and this repose and enthusiasm are not to be found in the vulgar atmosphere of crime and degradation, but in the contemplation of what is higher and better than ourselves.

There is nothing new in these principles. Long ago, the great German critic, Lessing, in "Laokoon," called the attention of the world to the fact that, among the ancients, beauty was the highest law of the imaginative arts. The masterpieces of the world have taught the same thing in every century; but it is necessary to repeat old truths again and again, just as it is necessary to teach the multiplication table to every new generation.

No one who has ever visited a museum in which the artistic productions of different nations are exhibited, can fail to have been struck with the progress from the ugly to the beautiful, as he passes from the works of the lower to those of the higher civilization. In the infancy of art, it is the grotesque, the repulsive, the monstrous that strikes the eye and is reproduced. To pass from the hideous masks of the Japanese to the perfect marbles of the Greeks, is to pass from barbarity to civilization, from ignorance to the highest culture. In the same manner, it is the gaudy and the tawdry that delight the ignorant, childish eye; it is not the soft melody, but the shriek of the penny whistle and the noise of the rattle that please his ear.

"I want something *awfully startling*," said a woman, standing near me, of a book-lender in one of our great city libraries. It wasn't difficult to please her. The manufacturers of the "awfully startling" are doing a good trade at present; but art? — Is there such a thing as going backward in art? There is, and it is against such retrogression that enlightened criticism is directed, and it is fitting that in France, where, more than in any other country, art has so far forgotten her

duty and aim as to deserve the severest reproaches and denunciations, criticism should
have reached a degree of perfection un-
equalled elsewhere. It is based, as we have
said before, on settled principles. It levies
contributions on all forms of human knowledge. It studies man and nature. It searches
the law beneath the action. It compares,
before it selects and judges. It knows the
value of the old observation that the truth
lies between extremes. It has discovered
what was wanting in the old idealists to
make them true seers, and what is wanting
in the new ultra-realism to make it fact.
The old idealists were constantly at war
with reality. The imagination played the
most important rôle in life. They searched
constantly to see that which is hidden, to
hear silence, to taste unknown joys. They
spurned the reality within reach, and spent
their lives in searching for the pot of gold
at the end of the rainbow, — over hills, over
valleys, not stooping to drink from the
brooks, when they were thirsty, for fear of
losing time; not wishing to gather the roses
by the wayside, for they knew that their
petals would quickly fall: and so they went
thirsty when they might have drunk, hungry

when they might have feasted, naked when they might have been clothed, weary when they might have rested, — and still the pot of gold waited — waited as it always will wait.   The one bugbear of these chimera-haunted creatures was materialism.   The flesh was but grass; the spirit was God.

Then came the reaction.   Flesh became God, and the spirit?   What am I? cried the sceptic.   Only an instrument upon which external forces play?   What is it that I can call myself?   The vibrating air brings me sound.   The vibrating ether gives me the conception of light.   Contact with matter brings me ideas of a non-ego, wonderful and varied.   Am I, after all, but a bundle of registered impressions?   And are these impressions registered in a perishable organ, my brain?   Is life but a conscious point in an eternity of unconsciousness?   If so, let me widen and deepen its consciousness by as many sensations as I can crowd into it.   But, alas! no quickening but rather deadening of consciousness follows the lawless satisfaction of the desires of the flesh.   "It hardens all within and petrifies the feeling."   Man is neither pure spirit nor pure matter.   He is soul and body, and each part of this dual

being properly claims recognition. Be his
life but a point in time, or an eternity, he
cannot taste the fulness of it here, without
obedience to the laws of his nature, the laws
of self-preservation, — morality.

It is the duty of criticism to assert this
dual nature of man; to allay, on the one hand,
our unreasonable fears of materialism, and,
on the other, to set the bounds to asceticism.
No criticism has done this so ably as French
criticism.   It stands neither for the ideal-
ism which is inaccessible, — the mysterious
"blue flower" that cannot be plucked, — nor
for the reality that is pure animalism.   It
is not sympathetic on the side of license
and emotionalism, nor on that of arbitrary
law and stoicism.   It stands for the free,
natural, healthy development of the normal
nature of man.   It stands for sunlight,
beauty, health, goodness, as opposed to darkness, ugliness, disease, and vice.   It believes
that art and literature have a duty to fulfil,
the duty of being a refuge and consolation
to the soul, and an inspiration to its noblest
development.